WORTHY
and
WANTED

TODD HOAGEY

WORTHY
and
WANTED

Know God.

Find Yourself.

Fulfill Your Purpose.

Copyright © 2021 by D. Todd Hoagey

All rights reserved, including the right to reproduce this book or portions thereof in any form whatsoever. No part of this publication may be reproduced or transmitted in any form or by any means, electronic or mechanical, including photocopying, recording, or any other information storage and retrieval, without the written permission of the author.

Unless otherwise indicated, all Scripture quotations are taken from the NIV Worship Bible, Copyright @1988 by Zondervan, Published by Zondervan, Grand Rapids, Michigan.

As indicated by CEV, Contemporary English Version (CEV) copyright 1995 by American Bible Society.

Hardcover ISBN: 978-1-63576-803-9
Paperback ISBN: 978-1-63576-762-9
eBook ISBN: 978-1-63576-805-3

Manufactured in the United States of America

0 9 8 7 6 5 4 3 2 1

Cover design by Charles Hames
Interior design by Neuwirth & Associates, Inc.

To my parents, Dave and Julia Hoagey.

Mom
For your spiritual awareness and inspiration, your persistence and patience, and for never giving up on me and my faith.

Dad
My best friend. Thank you for your unfailing love and support all my life, whether it was easy or not. I can't describe how comforting it is to know you are always there for me.

When God calls for your fulfillment of purpose,
reply respectfully, humbly, and dutifully,
and you, too, will be fulfilled.

CONTENTS

Introduction xi

PART 1 — MY JOURNEY

1. My Journey Around and Back 3
2. God's Embrace 15
3. Moving Forward 21
4. The Depths of Spirituality 25

PART 2 — YOUR JOURNEY

STEP 1. Awareness 35
STEP 2. Acceptance 47
STEP 3. Salvation 57
STEP 4. Communication 75
STEP 5. Relationship 101
STEP 6. Love 125
STEP 7. Trust 137
STEP 8. Obedience 157
STEP 9. Wisdom 177
STEP 10. Discernment 189
STEP 11. Fulfillment of Purpose 211

Wrapping It Up 231
Endnotes 235

INTRODUCTION

† "My teaching is not my own. It comes from him who sent me."
(John 7:16)

The Writings

Since Christmas morning, 2008, I've been writing notes in a private journal. I capture my innermost thoughts, concerns, questions, and prayers.

I also write words that are not my own. These entries are often in direct response to my personal notes, but other times are completely unsolicited. Sometimes I write little. Other times I fill pages with material. Some days I fully understand what I am writing. Other days I write out of obedience, like a scribe, trusting I will read later and learn the meaning of the messages. I believe these lessons are given to me directly from God. Actually, I hear from God, Jesus, and the Holy Spirit.

Let me clarify: I have not heard God's audible voice. I am referring to an inner voice, thoughts God plants during periods of quiet devotion. You will learn how this communication evolved in my life, and why I know it is also available for you.

Give God the glory! These lessons are not something I imagined; they are too profound for my analytical mind. I have no right to tell anyone anything about their life. I only present what I have been told. I was merely compelled by Jesus to write and share his good news.

For some of you, this may sound ridiculous! But, as you read through these lessons, you may become less skeptical and more receptive. If you are not aware of the possibility of a personal relationship with God, you are not alone. I was the same way. I went to church, considered myself religious, but my spiritual awareness never grew beyond Sunday worship! I spent my life learning about God instead of knowing him.

If you already believe God desires a relationship with us, this book may offer further affirmation. Use it as a compass for your own development. Use it as a guidebook to witness to others struggling with the concept.

I began to hear from God in 2008, and I continue to listen and learn every day. I wrote God's messages faithfully for ten years with no semblance of order or story. This book is a collection of those messages and experiences which were most impactful during my journey to know God. The random lessons were meaningful, but I did not understand the divine purpose. I was lost under a mound of snippets until I viewed the lessons topically instead of chronologically. When organized by subject matter, the eleven depths of spirituality emerged. God revealed the proper sequence for the steps, and the divine purpose became clear. His messages created a logical and thorough spiritual progression, offering insight into his nature and his desire for a relationship with us.

God's Voice

You will observe God's messages are delivered in simple, common prose. You may dismiss this as too ordinary for the God of the universe. You are absolutely correct! This is the beauty of his communication. You hear in terms you can easily understand. You will hear in your own language, using your own everyday words. God will not speak French to someone who only understands English or use words that are unfamiliar and require a dictionary.

Although you may hear clearly, you may not instantly and completely understand everything God says. Time or research is often necessary to fully internalize a message. But rest assured, you will not need a translator.

God often speaks directly to my heart in the first person. Other times, Jesus or the Holy Spirit delivers the message, either about God or on his behalf. This wisdom is about "Our Father." This clearly is not spoken by God but implies a third party is speaking. Jesus occasionally identifies himself, so I recognize his delivery, and this puts the message into the appropriate context.

I have no influence over the source of the messages. I usually don't notice a distinction until I reread my notes. I cannot explain how or why this happens. I simply allow myself to be open to hearing.

Don't let the messenger influence your perception of the importance of each message, for ultimately, all the messages are from God and are interchangeable.

The Opposition

I also write freely about Satan and the evil that exists in this world. There is scriptural evidence of Satan and his legions. Combat between the forces of good and evil is real. Spiritual warfare existed in biblical times and continues today!

Spiritual warfare may be unfamiliar or even disturbing, but to accurately present my complete Christian journey, it's necessary to include my series of learnings and experiences regarding the opposition. You will witness Satan attempting to disrupt my progress during my entire spiritual journey.

Making the Book

My story was inspired by God, but the road to completion was not easy. After I compiled the original manuscript, it was difficult finding a publisher.

Naively, I thought a Christian publishing house would be the best place to start. It turned out some Christian publishing companies would not consider a book professing God speaks directly to us. This is reserved for the Bible. For example, God speaking to Moses, or Jesus speaking to Saul, is acceptable to reference in a book, but to say God speaks to Todd, Joyce, Tarik, or anyone alive today, isn't theologically acceptable.

The Bible tells us God has spoken to many people throughout the Old Testament and the New Testament. We know it is possible! To say it is not theologically acceptable would imply either the Bible is a lie or that God has stopped communicating with people.

I believe the Bible is the word of God. It is God-breathed, it is true, it is the foundation for my faith. I am confident God still speaks with his people. Why would he stop? God doesn't have a speaking problem; we have a hearing problem!

A second publisher refused my manuscript, claiming Christians who do not hear from God may become offended by such claims and may doubt their own faith. I argue it's not a lack of faith, but a lack of information. My story may help others develop a relationship with God, which includes communicating directly with him. How can anyone learn of these opportunities with God if we are not permitted to write about them?

Maybe we should question our shallow commitment and faithless routines! Do we truly have the desire to fulfill God's purpose in our lives, or are we just going through robotic, religious motions, hoping our behavior is good enough to receive God's grace on judgment day?

My intent is not to present a systematic theology, although a book about relating and communicating with God ultimately takes me into theological territory. It is important to understand I wrote these messages as I lived them, without worrying about theological continuity or order received. There are experiences in the middle of the book that I learned recently, and earlier lessons that became relevant after developing a mature relationship with God, all supported by theological references when they occurred.

Although not by my design, much of the book is referenced with scriptural support. Many times, Bible verses were specifically shown to me to support God's teachings. It is a dual blessing and confirmation to learn from God and simultaneously be directed to a verse in the Bible, which perfectly coincides with his teachings. The joy I receive each time is absolute confirmation God validates what I hear, with a corresponding reference from his written Word.

Supporting scripture is sprinkled throughout God's messages and my personal notes with the symbol of a cross (†). I also include excerpts from other reference books, which I label **Insight**. During my quiet times with God, it was customary for me to open the Bible, the *Daily Guidepost* devotional, and generally one or two other books I was reading. These additional books were not written by God, but he used them to prove a point, supply inspiration, or validate theories or actions I was contemplating. Remarkably, I was often directed to a specific page in one of the books, meeting my exact needs at the time.

The messages in sans serif font are from God. In some instances, we conversed in real time in direct dialogue. But mostly, God chose the subject and taught the lesson, and I listened and learned. God also furnished the related scripture and insights to support his teachings in real time, which is why they appear sporadically throughout the book. You will see, however, the timing is far from random.

Some lessons may be hard to comprehend, particularly if you are new to the whole God thing. But I am confident as you read this book with an open mind, God will create understanding and reveal himself to you.

I witness what I heard and describe what I have experienced. I share the good news without judgment or conceit. I ask you to concentrate on God's words and make them relevant to your life, your spiritual journey, and your challenges.

This is a risky situation for me. I know naysayers will call me crazy. I'm okay with the skepticism. I know my experiences were real, and they continue today. I'm willing to accept criticism to further God's kingdom. I believe the positive feedback will outweigh the negative. The risk will be overshadowed by the satisfaction of knowing people were saved. I look forward to connecting with those whose lives are transformed by believing and ultimately developing an intimate relationship with God.

PART 1
My Journey

MY JOURNEY AROUND AND BACK

The Early Years

I GREW UP UNDER FAVORABLE CIRCUMSTANCES, in a typical family of four, bordering on privileged. We lived in a comfortable suburban township in Pennsylvania, nestled in the Amish countryside. Our middle-class neighborhood sprouted plenty of kids my age, a variety of playgrounds, and lots of thick green lawns.

Life was simple. Our community was safe; we could occupy ourselves without our folks worrying. Mom would call out the front door when it was time for dinner, and I would dart from someone's backyard. Every so often, I would need a little coaxing. Dad would yell for me, and a full sprint would ensue!

My parents have been married for over fifty years, and they still live in my childhood home. They don't drink or curse. My father worked two jobs, and my mother was a loving, stay-at-home mom for my younger sister and me. I always knew they loved me, and as a child, I never lacked anything.

I was a Boy Scout, enjoyed basketball, played whiffle ball in the streets, and avoided any serious trouble. I had no hardships to overcome unless I created them myself!

We attended church regularly, but I would not say religion played a big part in my life. I did not ask God to play a role in any decisions I made. I never thought of that!

In high school, I played sports every season, was student council president, and became an Eagle Scout. I always worked multiple jobs. My first three years of high school were so busy, I couldn't find time for trouble.

Then I became rebellious. I was a jerk in my last year of high school! I was accepted to Penn State University, and I was ready to move on. After basketball season ended in the spring, my grades tumbled. I knew everything and didn't need my parents anymore! I was sick of high school and this boring little hometown! I became frustrated and angry. My mother thought it would be tough to say goodbye to me when I went to college. But during this senior year of high school, she said I made it much easier for her to let me go!

Fast-forward two years to my first awareness experience. During our semester break from Penn State, a group of my college roommates and I traveled to meet each other for New Year's Eve. I remember this clearly because my favorite guitar-slinging hard-rock band was debuting its new video as the crystal ball dropped. We all wanted to witness the unveiling together, or maybe the video was just our excuse to get together and drink.

Music videos were a big deal in the 1980s. Before the internet, this was the only visual we had of musicians aside from live concerts. As a group, we had seen this band a couple of times in concert, so our anticipation was high. We huddled around the television as they started playing...the keyboard?!

I'm not sure whether I drank too many brews in anticipation of the video, or after, because of my disappointment with the band's apparent departure from hard rock. But my fog and headache the next day unmistakably signaled I, indeed, unfortunately, drank too much.

Mom sensed my discomfort from this indiscretion. I deserved a good sermon for this lack of good judgment, and for the other bad decisions

I made since my last year of high school. This time, Mom and Dad refrained from preaching. They were good at knowing when they needed to talk, and when I had learned my own lesson. This New Year's Day, apparently it was the latter.

Mom's cure for a hangover was not medicinal, but spiritual. She didn't say much to me as I lay on the couch. Instead, she gave me a copy of the book *He Came to Set the Captives Free* by Rebecca Brown, MD. I know I was vulnerable at the time, but this book scared me.

The book illustrates the horrifying tribulations of two women, Elaine and Dr. Rebecca Brown. For seventeen years, Elaine faithfully served Satan, driven by the lure of increased spiritual power, to become one of the most powerful and highest-ranking witches in the United States.

The author details the deception, torture, and sexual abuse Elaine and others endured at the hands of Satan. She describes Satan in frightening detail, along with his terrifying powers and indescribable hatred. She provides insight into the dark spirit realm and the prevalence of demons accessible only to those heavily involved in the occult.

Elaine eventually meets Dr. Rebecca Brown, an equally committed Christian and author of the book. Dr. Brown nearly loses her own life as she fights to rescue Elaine from Satan's stranglehold.

This was my introduction to the spirit world, to the evil in our society, to witches, demons, spiritual warfare, Satan, and the love and almighty power of Jesus. I'll never forget that day or the impact of this story on my life. This was an early awareness moment for me, a true spiritual awakening during a period of embarrassing personal weakness.

But I soon recovered from my headache and the shock from the book and returned to college.

I did not have time for religion. Despite God trying to show me the proper direction for my life, it would be twenty-some years before I would consider moving from awareness to acceptance and on to salvation. I simply got too busy. I did not make God a priority.

Following college, I married, moved to Deerfield Beach, Florida, bought a home, and started my first job, all within two months.

Immediately, I began my new life and career. Little did I know my career would quickly require five more relocations for six different employers.

I passed the certified public accountant (CPA) exam while working for a global public accounting firm. I was highly encouraged by the partners to bill two thousand hours per year to our clients. This is an aggressive goal, requiring a lot of overtime and weekends. This job lasted about three years.

I left the CPA firm to work in the private sector, but this second employer soon became insolvent.

I felt like I was hopping from canoe to canoe midstream when I quickly accepted job number three, a chief financial officer (CFO) position with a car dealership group. This position required me to commute an hour each way from Deerfield Beach to Stuart, Florida. After two years, we finally moved to Stuart to ease my daily drive.

Five years later, we were on the move again. I found work in downtown Fort Lauderdale and commuted nearly ninety miles each way for another two years before relocating again. I traveled extensively for this company and was then transferred to Rochester, New York.

Along with these career changes, we started a family. Having children added another dimension to our chaotic pace of life, travel, and moving. Our two boys were helplessly dragged along. Their childhood was much different from mine. They were constantly enrolling in new schools, finding and losing friends, and joining new sports teams. I regret the number of times they were uprooted and relocated.

This latest transfer was my fifth job, at age thirty-six. My family initially remained in Florida, while I moved to an apartment in Rochester. I was alone for a year, trying to decide whether to move my family again. We eventually bought a home in New York, and the pace of life continued at full throttle. Moving from Fort Lauderdale, Florida, to Rochester, New York, should have been my first indication I was placing too much emphasis on work! Who does this? Who moves from sunny South Florida to Rochester, New York?

As the boys got older, we participated in all the normal kid activities. Those included baseball and All-American Soap Box Derby racing throughout the northeast. My work intensified, and sports became a huge time commitment.

My last three jobs were start-ups, each in the retail car business. Anyone familiar with start-ups knows the time commitment required to make a new business successful!

I had now been going full tilt in the workforce for over thirty years, trying to maintain the same hectic pace I endured when I first began my professional career at age twenty-one. As I reflect, there were many warning signs which should have triggered a response to slow down.

I was always the last one to leave the office, the only one in the office on Saturday mornings. Always chasing the dream of success, never taking vacations. Time flew by quickly. Every job was fast-paced, demanded long hours, and created plenty of stress.

Then came the midlife crisis. Is there a time in everyone's life when we look in the mirror and ask questions like, "Who am I? Who have I become? What do I want to do with the rest of my life? Is this what I wanted to be when I grew up? Am I happy?"

I was not pleased with who I saw in the mirror, either physically, emotionally, or spiritually. I hit rock bottom spiritually. In fact, I had given up my faith. I was obviously not happy with my marriage of twenty-three years, because I was looking at other women, and I didn't know why.

My career had completely taken over my life. I was traveling more for work than was necessary, so I could escape the house and experience new adventures on my own. I wanted the freedom to be myself, which I had not known for years. Honestly, I had never been on my own as an adult.

I used to be happy…what happened?

I found myself out of town, working hard and playing harder, sleeping for a couple of hours and then going to work again. I went to the gym, lost weight, and updated my wardrobe. I was functioning like an eighteen-year-old. Although these behavioral changes may seem unusual, I started to feel alive again—energetic, personable, creative, and passionate about my life and my career. I felt like I got my personality back! I was looking good and feeling good, but I knew as a forty-four-year-old married man with children, I could not maintain this lifestyle for long.

† "Blessed is the man who always fears the Lord, but he who hardens his heart falls into trouble." (Prov 28:14)

Blinded by Darkness

We constantly face temptations. When we are young, it is harder to distinguish right from wrong because we have few experiences to draw from. As we grow older, our adventures become more dangerous. Sometimes we get away unscathed; other times, we aren't so lucky. My life lesson caught me by surprise and created a very dark period in my life, one I find difficult to discuss even now.

My wife and I married at a young age, and we made an oath to God to love each other until death do us part. For twenty years, our marriage was good. Hectic, but good. Seemingly overnight, I started making bad choices I knew were not healthy for my marriage.

If I had been a stay-at-home family man, I might have avoided trouble. But I did not. While out of town, I developed a relationship with a recently divorced woman. At this point, I had obviously given up on my marriage, but my wife was completely unaware.

When my wife discovered my betrayal, it was the most humiliating, regrettable moment of my life. She wanted to keep our marriage intact, but I was too far down the reckless path.

I spent the next five months wrestling with myself and mentally torturing my wife and two sons. I had become a miserable, ungodly person when I was at home, which was now amplified by the prevailing guilt and mistrust I caused.

I know my actions weren't justified, but my hardened heart continued to grow. It was an inexplicable feeling of indifference. I wasn't suicidal, but I was apathetic about everything. I just didn't care.

At the Lake

I needed to be alone for a while, so I could fix my inner conflict. Dejected but determined, I moved out of my house in September 2008 and signed a six-month lease for a house on a peaceful, beautiful lake not far from Rochester, New York.

Six months seemed like an appropriate amount of time to accomplish the tasks at hand. I needed to find myself, my spirituality, and then determine what was to become of my marriage, in that order. I was lost. I told my wife my soul felt black.

Only later did I realize six months was not nearly enough time, and there was no going back. Divorce was inevitable, but could I save myself? Could I find my spirituality and regain some joy in my life?

The rental house was a blessing from God. I know that now. It was exactly what I needed when I needed it. The four-thousand-square-foot home had a picturesque view of the lake from my living room and bedroom. The setting allowed me to stay home and feel content after years of restlessness. I did not feel confined or compelled to leave the house to find what I might be missing.

I refused to purchase a television. I wanted no distractions. The solitude allowed me to think. I was not on vacation; I had a purpose.

I cooked my own meals, cleaned the house as well as a man can, did my laundry, listened to music, and even found fulfillment planting flowers. I began to read. I hadn't read a book since college. I settled down into a reasonable pace with a clean, respectable lifestyle I found enjoyable and relaxing. I was accomplishing the first step—getting to know me again.

Discovering my spirituality and fixing my marriage were still untouched.

This troubled period in my life created a strenuous time with the boys. At this point, my oldest son was in college, and my younger son was a teenager in high school. My high schooler would visit on weekends, and we would spend quality time together on the lake, without worldly distractions, only him and me.

We bought a jet ski, built bonfires, cooked chicken breasts stuffed with cheese and bacon on the grill, created our own man-menu! I owned a couple of motorcycles, so we could ride together. It was a fun bonding time for the two of us. Quality was so much better than quantity, but I missed the quantity.

Despite the good times, a cloud of uncertainty hovered over our gatherings. Neither of the boys could possibly understand my inner turmoil, and we rarely talked about it. I was hopeful our bonds would not become irreparably damaged by my actions, but fear alone was not enough for me to turn back. I was resolved to fix myself and move on to spirituality.

I found a local church that was incredibly alive. This also, no doubt, was planned by God. Upon entering the sanctuary, I felt joy that could only be described as the Spirit of God. The singing, sermon, and fellow parishioners all exuded abounding enthusiasm. When the service was over, I wanted to stay! I felt like I could be a Christian and still enjoy life! Who knew!

I joined the church softball league. We prayed before the games. I never did that before! I was enjoying other Christians, and this new life was surprisingly comfortable.

I wanted to read the Bible. I purchased a new one, so I could mark it up, make notes, and personalize it. In three months, I read it from cover to cover. My craving to learn was insatiable.

I read dozens of books on all sorts of topics: spirituality, God, heaven, and hell. These books seemed to corroborate the lessons I was hearing in church, discovering in the Bible, or hearing on the radio. I was surprised how all the different influences (books, sermons, personal experiences) supported and confirmed each other with perfect timing.

I discovered Christian music, Christian rock specifically, and even Christian hard rock. I never knew there was such a thing! I could listen to my genre of music and not feel like I was sinning. What a wonderful new discovery!

The months flew past as I poured my energies into knowing God.

In December of 2008, I woke up alone Christmas morning. It was solemn. For the first time in my life, I was by myself on Christmas morning.

I went downstairs to the living room and lit a fire in the oversized, gray-stone fireplace. I made a cup of coffee, and with the softest, warmest blanket, I settled into my recliner, positioned with a perfect view of the lake and the fireplace. I had my Bible, a copy of the book *Listen, the Lord*, a blank writing journal, and my favorite pen.

I had nowhere to go and nothing to do. I sat quietly with my eyes closed and relaxed. I wrote "December 25, 2008" at the top of the first page of my newly purchased journal and included a segment from *Listen, the Lord* that I was reading: "I close the door of my spirit upon all except the words of God." I learned these words should be spoken to allow myself to fully concentrate on God, to block out all distractions and become receptive to hearing from God more clearly.

I was silent for a few minutes while contemplating these words when suddenly, I burst into uncontrollable weeping. With no one else home, it was easy to let the tears flow, to cry out loud, to freely allow myself to release all the fear, hopelessness, anger, self-pity, and pain. It was almost violent. I ignored all my inhibitions. There was no reason to hide my emotions and no one around to judge me. I didn't need to be concerned with embarrassing myself. In fact, in the beginning, I tried to control myself, and then I let go and gave my body over to my emotions.

I cried convulsively for an hour. I knew this was not an ordinary sob session. This was the turning point for my spirituality. I may have been physically purged of the darkness, through the expulsion of evil by God, as if the tears were God's gift of rain to cleanse my soul.

For the next two weeks, amid the chaos of holiday activities, I dedicated time to God with renewed enthusiasm. I felt connected, like a blockage had been removed. I was growing closer to God. God was my priority. I was excited about God.

Then on January 6, 2009, the next entry in the journal was not my own:

Don't be discouraged. Don't worry. I will come to you. Be persistent in your calling. Dedicate time for me every day. Be clear and hear my still, small voice.

On this day, I heard God. It was not an audible voice but an inner voice clearly not mine. If I had not been receptive to hearing from God, the message could easily have been missed or misinterpreted as my own. I knew they were not my own ideas because of the content. I knew I was spoken to, as opposed to speaking to myself. This is the only and best way I can describe it.

Afterward, as often as I could find the time, I faithfully turned to God, and he supplied a flow of thoughts and emotions I felt compelled to write down.

Months after my Christmas meltdown, following another episode of uncontrollable weeping, God led me to the following Bible verses and his subsequent message:

† "Streams of tears flow from my eyes, for your law is not obeyed." (Ps 119:136)

† "I open my mouth and pant, longing for your commands. Turn to me and have mercy on me, as you *always* do to those who love your name. Direct my footsteps according to your word, let no sin rule over me." (Ps 119:131–133, emphasis added)

Your heart is open to me, and I will fill it. The weeping is cleansing. The spiritual, scriptural reference is not coincidental.

Six months at the lake turned into two-and-a-half years. I received most of the messages included in this book during those years, along with the accompanying personal anecdotes and experiences.

I believed the lessons could be meaningful for others, so I began to share them with my parents and some close Christian friends. I shared them with my youngest son, who replied, "I feel like I'm reading the Bible."

Each one of these chapters was a new revelation for me. My emotional peaks and valleys are laid bare for you to see, firsthand, the ups, downs, and growing pains that accompany such a trek. You can follow my complete journey, both the good and the bad. It is a transformational experience.

Life Lesson Learned

As I reflect on the circumstances leading to my divorce, I realize I was stymied by a sense of complacency with my marriage. I was consumed with the concerns in my life, depressed about the lack of self-fulfillment, and certainly not focused on God. I was focused on myself, and I allowed the darkness that had so quickly crept in to overwhelm my life.

Not saying "No" to sin is the same as saying "Yes" to sin. Both responses say "Yes" to Satan. I lacked this foresight. I did not say "No" to Satan and didn't fight for my marriage. I accepted the inevitability of divorce.

I did not know the solution to save my marriage. I could not see the path to solving it. I see the path clearly now, and hopefully, God's revelation will continue through this book and reach all those facing similar difficulties.

All sin has consequences. I know my failure is not unique. Marriage is difficult. Many couples face the same challenges. For some, staying sober is difficult, or maybe avoiding drugs, gambling, pornography, other addictions, and other sins are hard to defeat.

For every predicament we create for ourselves, when we appeal to God with true remorse and seek his forgiveness, his grace will overcome our failure.

I believe God has forgiven me, and he made the best of my situation. He blessed me with a second chance at marriage, a wonderful, loving wife, two beautiful daughters, and a relationship with his son Jesus.

It's not too late to ask God for forgiveness, healing, and redemption. Don't be blinded by the darkness, consumed by your circumstances. Take control of your future. He is waiting for you. You are worthy and wanted by God.

It is possible for you to complete this life-changing journey. You will not take the trip by yourself; you will not be alone. I am a witness God desires to share your journey. My purpose is to deliver this message to you. Embark on the journey that will change your life.

GOD'S EMBRACE

† "I love the Lord, for he heard my voice; he heard my cry for mercy. Because he turned his ear to me, I will call on him as long as I live." (Ps 116:1–2)

THE FOLLOWING MESSAGES FROM GOD gave me insight into his caring and forgiveness. His messages are never condemning but always loving and understanding. Everything is under control, and the timing for everything is according to God's plan. It is extremely comforting, like a big loving embrace.

I felt tremendous guilt approaching God after all my years of sporadic Christianity, which is probably why God addressed this elephant in the room first.

Welcome Back

We started this journey when you were at your worst. You wrote me off, and now you are writing for me. You said, "I know God exists, and I don't care." I heard you. You were as far away as you could be. You believed in me; you just denied me. I waited a long time to speak with you.

Do not condemn yourself. I do not condemn you. Do not fear for a minute that your absence diminished our chance to have a relationship. Satan wants you to think you have no hope. You have been faithful to come back to me.

We have begun to build a foundation of faith, and it is very strong. Rejoice in your progress. Take time to reflect and appreciate what we have done together.

The missing years have not been wasted; you have a lifetime ahead of you. I don't care about the past. You are here now. I am glad you have come back to me with such determination. Rejoice and be glad we are together. The Holy Spirit is with me always and with you. He is in constant communication. Therefore, you are not absent. You were never absent.

GOD'S EMBRACE — PERSONAL REFLECTION

I CAN RELATE TO THE parable of the prodigal son from the son's perspective; to some extent, I have been through these highs and lows. I also understand from the forgiving father's perspective, as I have witnessed God's grace firsthand.

This parable is powerful on many levels, from the son's confession, repentance, and humility to his father's unconditional forgiveness.

The Parable of the Prodigal Son

Here is the parable Jesus told about the wayward son in Luke 15:11–24:

> Jesus continued: "There was a man who had two sons. The younger one said to his father, 'Father, give me my share of the estate.' So he divided his property between them.
>
> Not long after that, the younger son got together all he had, set off for a distant country, and there squandered his wealth in wild living. After he had spent everything, there was a severe famine in that whole country, and he began to be in need. So he went and hired himself out to a citizen of that country, who sent him to his fields to feed pigs. He longed to fill his stomach with the pods that the pigs were eating, but no one gave him anything.

When he came to his senses, he said, 'How many of my father's hired men have food to spare, and here I am starving to death! I will set out and go back to my father and say to him: "Father, I have sinned against heaven and against you. I am no longer worthy to be called your son; make me like one of your hired men."' So he got up and went to his father.

But while he was still a long way off, his father saw him and was filled with compassion for him; he ran to his son, threw his arms around him, and kissed him. The son said to him, 'Father, I have sinned against heaven and against you. I am no longer worthy to be called your son.'

But the father said to his servants, 'Quick! Bring the best robe and put it on him. Put a ring on his finger and sandals on his feet. Bring the fattened calf and kill it. Let's have a feast and celebrate. For this son of mine was dead and is alive again; he was lost and is found.' So they began to celebrate.

* * *

This parable reveals God's forgiveness and acceptance of his children, despite our rebellion and disobedience.

The young man is given everything in life, including his father's inheritance. He exercises the freedoms he always wanted to experience, albeit immorally and consequently squanders everything. The son did not immediately run home when the wealth was gone; he went to work on a farm and was so hungry he longed to eat pig food!

How stubborn do we get? How humble must we become before we ask for help? How long do we wait, when faced with adversity, before we turn to God? Until we envy the pigs in the field?

Scripture says prior to going home, the young son planned to confess to his father, prepared to become his father's servant (Luke 15:18–19). He did not know how his father would receive him. This is important because it demonstrates the honest intent of the young man; his realization of having done what is wrong, his sincere humility, and his desire to come clean with his father. He was out of options and was prepared for the consequences.

As he approached home and his father compassionately welcomed him, the son still confessed, even though it appears it may not have been necessary. The prodigal son said he was not worthy and was prepared to be a servant. He followed through with his planned confession.

The father demonstrated his unconditional love and forgiveness by graciously receiving his son even before the son confessed. How did he know his son's intent? He could have been coming home to get more money!

When the father finds his son, it doesn't matter what the son did, what the son looks or smells like, or his excuses for doing what he did. The reason for his return is irrelevant to the father. All that matters to the father is that the son had been lost, and now, he is found.

God knows our heart, knows our intent, and welcomes us with unconditional forgiveness. Time, distance, and behavior are not important. God is waiting with open arms for us to return, so he can embrace us, forgive us, and celebrate!

3

MOVING FORWARD

GOD WELCOMED ME BACK, AND our relationship began. It was time to get to work.

At the beginning of my journey, I had no idea it was going to be a journey. I received a few short messages, and I was thrilled. As I spent more time with God, the communication became more intense. Every day was a surprise, a new topic which elevated my understanding. I lived day by day, lesson by lesson, enjoying each new revelation without knowing where it was leading.

The following messages from God describe three distinct stages of my journey.

* * *

In the beginning, God delivered reassurance of his plan and encouraged me to spend more time with him. He was more concerned with my learning than my writing. Writing a book was nowhere on my radar. My purpose was to spend time with God consistently and experience the maturation of this new relationship.

Rest in me. Allow me to give you peace. This calm, during everything going on in your life, is from me. It's a calm you won't want to leave.

Continue to read my Word every day. You need this scriptural foundation. Make these readings part of your mornings, even if only for a moment.

Learn what you can about my son and his love. You must have his love and feel his love in order to share it with others. Speak to Jesus and allow him to be a part of you.

Do not force communication for communication's sake. Find alternative ways of worship and fellowship. Read the Bible. Maybe today's message is there. The power of fellowship includes reading the Bible, interacting with other Christians, praying, being quiet and still. All are equally important and fulfilling. These are all ways to feel my love.

Worship does not have to be limited to a time slot in the morning with a pen and paper. It is easy to be in my presence during the day. You can find my peace anywhere. I come to you as often as you come to me because I love you. Worship me with your thoughts and songs, and you will feel joy.

Do not frustrate yourself with periods of silence. Be persistent and fight through the periods when you feel our communication is lacking. Do not doubt my intention to speak to you or your ability to hear from me. This is of Satan. Cast away doubt in the name of Jesus Christ and move on.

Tomorrow is brand-new, like an unopened present. Who does not open a present for fear of what's inside? It will bring change, it will be new, it is a gift from me. Open tomorrow, and each day, like a new present. You are starting your life anew, physically and spiritually. Experience both with equal passion and enjoy.

You want to know what I have in store for you so you can plan. It is for me to plan. Do not worry yourself with assisting me. Continue to study and learn and experience. I will do the rest. Do not waste a single minute planning, just be aware of my workings around you and be receptive.

* * *

During the second phase, God extended his promise of support and fellowship going forward. He hinted at revealing his purpose in his time when he felt I was ready for the next step.

I have a definite plan for you. Keep your faith in me, and not yourself, to blaze the trail. My road will not be easy. You will be constantly challenged, led by me. Give me the burden of the journey's mapping, and be willing to travel the path.

Do not be stressed about writing a book. Do not worry about works right now. Don't let the writing get in the way of your hearing, or apply so much pressure on the writing that you miss me. It is easy to get caught up with obedience and fulfillment of purpose. People get consumed by doing deeds and lose their original source of inspiration—me!

When I want you to do more for me, I will lead you, and make it obvious. I know you are impatient. I know your doubts and skepticism. I know what type of prodding you require. I know your capabilities and desires. I also know your challenges and limitations. I work to increase the former and reduce the latter until you are ready.

Do not ask where this is leading, but ask, "What is the next step?"

You did not come to me initially with the intent of gaining wisdom to write a book and witness on my behalf. This is not your design. This is a desire I placed in your heart as a result of our relationship. I understand your willingness and will not waste your interest. When the time is right, we can work quickly. You will see the purpose in your notes, and it will be a grand story.

You have been led to this juncture carefully. When the time comes to take the next step, you will know, and you will be ready. You do not know what miracles I may be performing to pave the way for your future.

* * *

God encouraged me to write in the third stage, which occurred two years later. At this point, I had several journals full of God's messages,

Bible verses, and collections of my own thoughts and experiences. I felt they should be shared, but did not know if God agreed.

Your desire to help me is pleasing. Most look to me to help themselves. You prefer to help others; you have always been this way.

Look at your beginning and compare it to where you are today. You were lost. You had no direction, no knowledge, and certainly, no sense of duty like you do now.

You look for signs to move forward. I ask you to proceed and be aware of my guidance and cautions, for I will give both to protect you and your work for me.

Begin to write the book you envision. Write with all the passion in your heart. You are experiencing an intense period of teaching and learning wonderful lessons that I, without a doubt, want you to share.

You are writing lessons to lay out the future for those willing to listen. They impact the audience I need to reach today.

I am not interested in religion. I am interested in a relationship. I want to bring joy and peace to my children now. It isn't all about eternity. Live life for today and eternity. Live with my love now, on earth. This is the message I want to deliver to you, and I want you to deliver it to the world.

* * *

All three of these messages from God offered comfort and clarity during the most difficult times of my journey. He lovingly guided my quest to learn his purpose for my life, including whether I should spend what I suspected would take lots of time and effort writing a book.

THE DEPTHS OF SPIRITUALITY

THE JOURNEY BEGINS HERE, WITH the eleven depths of spirituality. Following years of journaling, God revealed the order to present his lessons. Even after this sequence was penned, God continued to reinforce his messages with ongoing support and experiences. I hear pastors preaching today as if they've read this book, and it's not published yet.

Remember, I was not highly spiritual prior to my personal experiences documented here. I'm an accountant by trade. So, these lessons imparted to us, through me, would have been impossible for me to develop on my own. But these ongoing confirmations gave me the confidence to invite you to follow this journey with me, knowing God intends all of us to read and learn and grow closer in our relationship with him.

* * *

✝ "The Lord would speak to Moses face to face, as a man speaks with his friend." (Exod 33:11a)

Evidence of God's direct communication and fellowship with folks on earth is documented in the Old Testament. In the New Testament, Jesus created this opportunity for each of us with his sacrifice on the cross and God's blessing of the Holy Spirit.

God desires to have a relationship with us today! He reveals in the following overview *how* this relationship can evolve, the logical succession of intimacy, and the joyous benefits available during our lifetime on earth. It's one thing to say a relationship is possible with God, but it's entirely different to figure out how this relationship materializes.

You can call this spiritual progression a series of steps or milestones, whatever is comfortable for you. The purpose of this book is to share God's messages regarding how to start a relationship and how the journey involves each of the following advances of spiritual development. Internalize these spiritual milestones, and give God the opportunity to perform the steps with you, in your life.

INSPIRATION FROM GOD

Ponder the following spiritual milestones. Within each milestone, there are numerous levels of achievement. Spiritual maturity comes from maximizing each milestone, not racing to the end.

The milestones serve as a road map for anyone beginning the journey. When you read a map, you are not shown all the road signs, construction zones, and speed limits. You only experience those aspects of the trip after you actually start the journey.

1. Awareness
2. Acceptance
3. Salvation
4. Communication
5. Relationship
6. Love
7. Trust
8. Obedience
9. Wisdom
10. Discernment
11. Fulfillment of purpose

The Depths of Spirituality—Jesus Inspired

I have given you the directions; now follow the path with unfailing faith and confidence and fulfill your purpose!

People write books who have far less knowledge than you. People preach with far less spirituality than you. There are people who prophesy who have heard less than you. You see how important you could be to me?

I am tasking this to you because you understand. You are a good translator. You are an encourager and a persuader. Persuade people to follow me. Teach the steps. Give people the awareness and desire. I will supply the means and the way.

Who better to write a book about the steps in a spiritual journey than one who is taking the steps one by one, day by day, not knowing what tomorrow brings? You are a clean canvas for me. You write passionately because everything is new to you.

When words don't exactly illustrate your point, God will give the appropriate interpretations. God works in the most perfect ways.

How satisfying would it be to do God's work on earth, knowing he will lead your every step, and take away all your worries? God's presence isn't just to get you through this life; he also wants you to enjoy this life to the fullest.

Few people speak of spirituality in a practical sense. Most teach the law, and the law needs to be taught! But the spirituality I describe is alive. It is progressive. It is not condemning and divisive, like the old law. This spiritual intimacy allows us to grow closer together, to love and enjoy life without the fear of retribution.

THE DEPTHS OF SPIRITUALITY—
PERSONAL REFLECTION

GOD DESIRES A RELATIONSHIP WITH us. He provides clear direction, with spiritual milestones as markers. The first three steps must happen in this order:

1. Awareness
2. Acceptance
3. Salvation

You must first be aware God exists. It's impossible to achieve the second milestone, acceptance, if you've never become aware of God's existence. You then have a choice—either accept or reject God. He wants you to accept what you have learned, consider it to be the truth, and believe without fully understanding. When you develop this faith, you will be motivated to ask for forgiveness of your sins and seek salvation.

Look at the entire list of eleven milestones and notice where salvation appears; quite close to the top! This is where many people feel the relationship with God culminates! On the contrary, salvation is only the beginning! Certainly, salvation is the most significant milestone, but it was never intended to be the end goal. It should not be the end of the journey but the beginning of a relationship.

The sad part is many people never progress further than awareness. How many people "want to someday" but are too busy right now? Do they think the commitment is too great? Have more important priorities? How many people do not make the decision to be saved? I lived for many years bound by these excuses. For numerous reasons, it took me twenty-three years between awareness and salvation.

When you enter into a relationship with God, you begin a lifelong journey together. After salvation, the milestones continue:

4. Communication
5. Relationship
6. Love
7. Trust
8. Obedience
9. Wisdom
10. Discernment
11. Fulfillment of Purpose

You may say that not everything happens in this specific order. Maybe it hasn't for you, and maybe it won't. But the steps outline a logical progression of intimacy and correspond closely to the evolution of a human relationship; they lead to one another and depend on each other. Review the order of events; isn't communication usually important to form a good friendship? Loving someone is hard without first having some sort of relationship. It's easier to trust someone you love, and it is more palatable to be obedient when there's trust.

Wisdom, discernment, and fulfillment of purpose sound more divine than human. They can certainly evolve with the maturity of an earthly relationship as well but are actually fruits of a vibrant life with God. Because of your communication, relationship, love, trust, and obedience, God grants the virtues of wisdom, discernment, and fulfillment of purpose.

His wisdom far exceeds any possible knowledge we would have without his guidance, including valuable insights into our personal behavior and personality traits.

Discernment between good and evil is crucial as you pursue the ultimate objective of fulfilling God's purpose for your life. You certainly want to distinguish whether you are being led by God or by Satan!

These steps are not milestones to be achieved and then discarded like old trophies. It's not a checklist. You don't get one done and move to the next level. They are constantly revisited and built upon like foundation stones joined together to construct and support a house. God decides when you are ready to advance, and only he can lead the way.

* * *

The Bible contains all we need to know for salvation and for godly living, but it is only a fraction of God. Although it is God's Word, it certainly is not all of God—the same as these notes are part of me but not all of me. There is so much more to God than what is written in the 929 chapters and sixty-six books of my Bible.

John 21:25 reveals, "Jesus did many other things as well. If every one of them were written down, I suppose that even the whole world would not have room for the books that would be written."

This step-by-step handbook reveals a clear path for developing a living relationship with God. Hopefully, through these messages, you will gain a deeper awareness of God's love and become confident in his desire to have a close relationship with you.

PART 2
Your Journey

STEP 1

AWARENESS

† "Jesus answered, 'I am the way and the truth and the life. No one comes to the Father except through me.'" (John 14:6)

God Speaks About Jesus

Jesus is my son, with whom I am well pleased, as I am with you. He is the child; I am the Father. Those who know my son, know me.

No one comes to me except through my son Jesus. Through Jesus, our fellowship is possible. Jesus is the light, the joy, comfort, and peace you feel. Jesus walked in your shoes and continues to forevermore. He is everlasting love and forgiveness. He is the one with the patience for you!

Pray in Jesus's name. Call on him during your prayer time. He is the petitioner, he is the counselor, he is the victor. He is a teacher, as you will be.

We know the challenges and complexities of the world. We sympathize with your dilemmas, with your constant earthly battles. We give you the solution: Jesus.

You want to proclaim boldly you love Jesus, but you feel uncomfortable. You will learn your love for Jesus is not something you develop, but something he develops within you, arising from your obedience and the maturation of your relationship.

Do not think of loving Jesus in the human context of love; it is not earthly love. This is spiritual love. Ask the Holy Spirit to reveal the roadblocks preventing you from feeling close to Jesus.

Demonstrate your love for Jesus through your appreciation and commitment to follow him. This relationship will continue to mature, and you will eventually, naturally, love Jesus.

The Holy Spirit Speaks About Jesus

Picture Jesus praying on your behalf, kneeling before God and pleading, speaking your name, asking for help for your challenges! This is what Jesus does when he knows you.

Jesus is the way.

Learn about Jesus, learn from him, live for him.

Jesus is love. His love wins wars.

Jesus is the Word. He brought the word of God to the world.

Jesus is God. He never sinned. He was, is, and always will be.

Jesus is the benchmark. Do not look at others and judge yourself by their standards.

Jesus is your companion. In everything you do, he is there. Feel his presence.

You can have a wonderful, everlasting relationship with Jesus.

In the name of Jesus Christ, anything is possible.

Jesus Speaks About Jesus

† "I no longer call you servants. Instead, I have called you friends, for everything that I learned from my Father I have made known to you." (John 15:15)

Jesus is my name. Use my name when you pray. Call on me by name, and you will know me better. Those who believe in me are accepted by the Father.

I love you, my child. Relax and feel my presence. You have learned a lot about me in a short time. I hear your prayers. I will provide for you.

I can be your best friend. The friend who will never leave you. The friend who will not judge. A friend who forgives. Trust me as your friend for protection, for guidance, for love. Say my name for peace and thanksgiving.

The more you call on me, the more you will know me. You will feel me. You will see me everywhere in your life! You will know I am with you.

Find peace in me, then joy. True peace and joy and love come from me. You cannot exude joy if you do not have joy. Find joy in your life through me, your friend, your savior Jesus Christ. Joy and love go hand in hand. Can you have one without the other?

Look at me differently. I was on the earth like you. I cried human tears, I laughed, I loved. Trust I know all you are feeling. All you need is me; I can do anything.

Three in One

God the Father—Jesus the Savior—Holy Spirit the Comforter.

These are the three legs of the Trinity and the sources of love, grace, and fellowship. You cannot receive the love of God from anyone but God. You cannot receive the grace of God from anyone but Jesus. You cannot receive fellowship with God from anyone but the Holy Spirit.

Jesus Speaks About the Holy Spirit

✝ "But when he, the Spirit of truth, comes, he will guide you into all truth. He will not speak on his own; he will speak only what he hears, and he will tell you what is yet to come. He will bring glory to me by taking from what is mine and making it known to you." (John 16:13–14)

✝ "In the last days, God says, I will pour out my Spirit on all people." (Acts 2:17a)

The Holy Spirit is the gift from God. The gift that can only come from him! His presence will grow stronger in your life as you allow him. He is a powerful presence, and you will sense his guidance. The Holy Spirit is God on earth. The Holy Spirit is the conduit between heaven and earth. Prayer is powerful when performed with the help of the Holy Spirit.

The joy you feel in church is the Holy Spirit coming alive within you. These virtues are evidence of the Spirit in you. You will feel this joy in your everyday life and know it is a gift from God.

To abide in the Holy Spirit, you must have discipline over the flesh. In this regard, we will help you if you let us. Continue to seek the guidance of the Holy Spirit and expect to see improvement in your awareness. The Holy Spirit within you has been awakened.

God Speaks About the Holy Spirit

> ✝ "Peter replied, 'Repent and be baptized, every one of you, in the name of Jesus Christ for the forgiveness of your sins. And you will receive the gift of the Holy Spirit.'" (Acts 2:38)

It is I, the Father, who hears you. It is I who instructs the Holy Spirit. It is my Spirit given to you. Our spirits are united. Be still and feel the Holy Spirit. He is constantly praying on your behalf.

Strengthen your fellowship with the Holy Spirit. Start your time by engaging the Holy Spirit in the morning, and your time will be blessed. Your wisdom will grow deeper, and your insight will be more obvious.

Ask the Holy Spirit for guidance in evaluating your circumstances and options, and you will get better at recognizing the doors I open for you and the ones you open out of your own free will. The Holy Spirit will apply subtle pressure to actions in your life. Recognize those urges and evaluate the source. Because you have free will, you will make decisions that please me, and others that are not pleasing. You will know which are which based on how you feel inside. You will feel joy or disappointment. These feelings will grow stronger with an increased presence of the Holy Spirit. Rejoice in his presence, for the feelings of joy will far outweigh the feelings of disappointment.

Ask the Holy Spirit to help you pray for the longings of your heart. When you love me with all your heart, the longings of your heart will also be mine.

Invite the Holy Spirit to participate actively in your life. He will react to your attention; he will delight in your fellowship. The more attention you give him, the more attention he will give you.

AWARENESS—
PERSONAL REFLECTION

Awareness has been delivered! Consider yourself aware! You've been given a firsthand explanation of the Trinity, and profound wisdom from God, Jesus, and the Holy Spirit. The first milestone has been achieved!

For a long time, I did not feel like I knew Jesus. I did not recognize the difference between God the Father and Jesus. I did not understand how the Holy Spirit fit into the mix. Should I pray to God or Jesus? The concept of the Trinity was intellectually challenging.

This is a powerful series of messages intended to clarify the roles of the Trinity. The doctrine of the Trinity is fundamental to Christians. It is important to believe in this seemingly impossible situation, to understand how God works, and how we can interact with him.

God is three distinct beings; God the Father, God as the son Jesus, and God's Holy Spirit——all is one God; all have a distinct purpose and are available to help us.

The existence of the Trinity raises many questions that, quite frankly, no one can answer because we cannot comprehend. There is no way to adequately explain the Trinity, and many have tried. As Christians, we only learn what we can from the Bible.

> ✝ "May the grace of the Lord Jesus Christ, and the love of God, and the fellowship of the Holy Spirit be with you all." (2 Cor 13:14)

There are many verses that reveal God as Father (1 Pet 1:2), (John 6:27); Jesus as God (Rom 9:5), (Col 2:2, 9); and God's Holy Spirit (1 Cor 3:16), (Acts 5:3–4). There is one God (Isa 46:9) who displays himself in three persons.

God's Existence

I am confident all humans are exposed to the concept of God at some point in their lives, somehow. Paul confirms that people must first become aware of God's existence.

> ✝ "How, then, can they call on the one they have not believed in?
> And how can they believe in the one of whom they have not heard?
> And how can they hear without someone preaching to them?"
> (Rom 10:14)

Awareness is the reason for missions, Christian outreach in communities, fans holding John 3:16 signs behind the backstop at baseball games, street preachers in New York City, and fish-shaped bumper stickers. God uses all these means to reveal himself.

How can God hold someone accountable for not accepting Christ if they have never been made aware of his existence? This awareness is the first step toward salvation.

Different awareness experiences may come together, prompting you to seek more information so you can make an informed opinion and accept the truth. For me, there was one defining "aha" moment. It came when I was unsure about taking communion.

My First Communion

When I was a kid, Mom did her best to wake the family and drag us to the neighborhood Presbyterian church. But Sunday school for kids was only one step removed from babysitting.

When I attended worship services in the sanctuary with my parents, my fondest memories involve goofing off with Dad. We would elbow each other, mimic each other's movements, and giggle. Otherwise, I didn't like church much. The sermons were too intellectual for me, it was boring, and I had other stuff to do.

When I myself became an adult and parent, I didn't know what my Christianity should look like. I barely understood the principles of being a Presbyterian. When someone would ask my religion, I would answer, "Protestant," not knowing if Presbyterian was a religion. Was I Presbyterian? A Protestant? Was there a difference? What other choices are available?

I knew Holy Communion was a revered tradition in Catholicism. I was also vaguely aware of the incense, rosaries, and Hail Marys, none of which I understood or perceived as Bible-based. I attended Catholic services periodically with friends, but these rituals made me uncomfortable. Maybe I simply did not understand Catholicism, but in my mind, I lumped all these practices together and viewed them with skepticism, as they were different from my upbringing.

This may seem strange for someone writing a book on how to have a relationship with God, but even in my mid-thirties, I was still remarkably naive about religion.

Shortly after our first son was born, we attended a Congregational church in Florida. We were visiting this church for the first time after moving to town. At the end of the service, communion was offered. I started sweating. I didn't know whether taking communion was the right thing to do! What did I get myself into? I looked for the exits. The pastor seemed like a nice enough guy. The service was comfortable. I didn't feel like I was worshipping the devil! If this was the wrong thing to do, would God forgive me? What was a Congregational church, anyway? Was I allowed to take communion? Was I supposed to take communion? Was this a Catholic church? What should I do? Where was that exit?!

I closed my eyes and lowered my head, and instantly I saw a vision of my mother taking communion. God knew my confusion, and he gave me a vision…the only vision which could have thoroughly convinced me, without a doubt, I was supposed to take communion. It was a remarkable supernatural event in my life I will never forget—my first vision. My mother was the symbol of Christianity in my life, and seeing her take communion, in my mind, was perfect validation communion was a good thing. More impressive is the fact I never remember seeing my mother take communion in real life.

God can deliver the most perfect messages, in the most convincing fashion, in the most unusual ways, with perfect timing.

I not only participated in communion that day, but as an eventual church member, I prepared the communion elements the first Sunday of every month for several years.

This vision occurred in adulthood and was impactful because it was God-generated, yet custom-tailored for me. It was also significant because I became aware of visions, a phenomenon I did not know existed. It was delivered so perfectly, I realized the source had to be God.

Despite this miracle, I eventually returned to the busyness of life and forgot about God.

Moving from Awareness to Acceptance

Now, with all this information about awareness, you must weigh the option of whether to accept it as truth or not. Read the Bible. Let God lead you to believe. If you continue to be curious, it's a good sign God is working in you.

Curiosity will drive you to learn more. Find a church that is alive. Join groups with people of similar spiritual maturity. Ask questions of your pastor or find a spiritual mentor.

My spiritual mentor was a bellwether of truth and reason when I began to hear from God. We dissected my fragmented messages every week. Her encouragement helped when I questioned my direction. She listened patiently and confirmed my awareness as I described my spiritual progress. She was also an oasis of peace in the midst of my marriage turmoil.

She was extremely helpful in my spiritual and personal development. As I grew spiritually, I experienced many changes personally. The most significant benefit was gaining confidence in my new faith, bold with my Christianity.

My mentor confirmed my awareness and made me secure in my acceptance of God's presence in my life. Since you are now aware, pray for better understanding and move on to acceptance.

STEP 2

ACCEPTANCE

ACCEPTANCE IS THE DECISION TO believe in God and accept his offering. You have a choice. No matter how far from God's path you stray, God will draw you back to the warmth of his love when you accept his invitation.

† "For God so loved the world that he gave his one and only Son, that whoever believes in him shall not perish but have eternal life." (John 3:16)

† "Then you will know the truth, and the truth will set you free." (John 8:32)

Everyone Will Have a Choice

Awareness must be recognized before acceptance can be realized.

Everyone is given an opportunity to accept me or reject me; either believe or not believe. You choose what you will. I offer the opportunity of a lifetime and give people the choice.

Satan works hard to stifle the broadcasting of this opportunity to minimize its importance. Satan would like you to think no choice is necessary!

Believe you have a choice. Those who choose to believe receive life, both now on earth, and later in heaven.

Why do people resist me, when all I offer is love? The busyness of life is the biggest deterrent. They do not make an effort to prioritize me. There are too many other decisions in life that take precedence.

Don't you make every effort to show your children what is important? What is right? If at first, they make the wrong decision, would you not grant them every opportunity to make the right decision, regardless of the number of attempts?

My grace, mercy, and forgiveness are available to everyone at no cost. There is no expiration date. There are not a limited number of attempts. All have this promise. Make the choice to accept these gifts from me.

Choose God's Path — Jesus Inspired

† Always let him lead you, and he will clear the road for you to follow. (Prov 3:6 CEV)

Follow in my footsteps, my child. My footsteps are laid out forever. You may choose to walk in them or blaze your own trail. Don't fear where my footsteps are leading. Trust me and step in them. Take one step at a time and stay close behind me. If you stumble and fall, I will be there to pick you up.

It is night, in a snowstorm, and you cannot find your own way. How much easier is it to walk in someone else's footprints in the deep snow? Know the storm will lessen and eventually pass, the sun will shine, and the warmth will be great. Then we will walk on the beach, where following in footsteps is easy and fun.

You will know me as your friend. This is how you will love me. I will be with you always, and you will know I am there. Weather the storm by accepting my help, choosing my path.

People Want to Believe

† "They replied, 'Believe in the Lord Jesus, and you will be saved—you and your household.'" (Acts 16:31)

† "Yet to all who received him, to those who believed in his name, he gave the right to become children of God...born of God." (John 1:12–13)

† "And without faith it is impossible to please God, because anyone who comes to him must believe that he exists and that he rewards those who earnestly seek him." (Heb 11:6)

The world needs encouragement to believe in me. Undeniable belief is the key. Belief comes from your heart convincing your brain; knowing, not thinking.

Many people switch churches, denominations, and religions, searching for spiritual satisfaction. They want to believe, but they can't find the right inspiration on Sunday mornings. Others rely too heavily on Sundays to sustain their belief. They don't trust me to lead their lives during the week or think of me on a daily basis.

Is there infallible proof the Bible is God's Word? Is there undeniable proof Jesus was my son? Is there evidence I even exist? The answer is no. You must believe, and through belief, you will be taught the truth.

Receive my gifts and my salvation. My blessings wait for you to accept.

ACCEPTANCE — PERSONAL REFLECTION

How often do you hear, "I don't believe in God"? These folks acknowledge they are aware of God but have chosen not to accept him. They have weighed the evidence and chosen not to believe.

This is the proverbial fork in the road. Everyone who travels down the path must decide to take the right path or the wrong path. We dictate the direction. If we choose the right path, God leads the way. Many are deceived, thinking the wrong path is right.

Many believe no choice is necessary or is not necessary at this time. They can deal with this choice later; they are too busy right now. Surely God will understand. This procrastinator was me!

Satan is the deceiver. He is the prince of the earth. Satan hates God, and I believe he also hates us. This fork in the road is Satan's last stand. If we choose to go to the right, Satan loses since he knows salvation is the next step. He creates busyness to distract humanity, preventing us from choosing the right or making a choice at all. We spend hours surfing the internet, keeping up with social media, watching television; all preventing us from making a choice because we don't have time. We're too busy.

I'm amused by people who say, "I didn't have time to do that today." What they should say is, "I chose not to do that today because I did not make it a priority." *Prioritize your time!* Make the right choice at the fork in the road and accept God's invitation.

Consider all who choose the wrong path, thinking it is okay. Society has been tricked into thinking there's nothing wrong with the wrong path! Many are choosing this path because their decisions are being supported by the great deceiver's manipulation of right versus wrong in today's world. The uncensored internet and the promiscuity and immorality on television and radio present a distorted view of what's normal and is not perceived as sinful. People think if it's shown on TV, it must be okay. They are choosing the wrong path because it appears mainstream and acceptable.

It is not too late to realize your mistake, accept God, repent, and receive his forgiveness.

The Parable of the Great Banquet

Jesus told the following story about an invitation to a banquet while dining at the house of a religious leader (Luke 14:16–24):

> Jesus replied: "A certain man was preparing a great banquet and invited many guests. At the time of the banquet he sent his servant to tell those who had been invited, 'Come, for everything is now ready.'
>
> But they all alike began to make excuses. The first said, 'I have just bought a field, and I must go and see it. Please excuse me.'
>
> Another said, 'I have just bought five yoke of oxen, and I'm on my way to try them out. Please excuse me.'
>
> Still another said, 'I just got married, so I can't come.'
>
> The servant came back and reported this to his master. Then the owner of the house became angry and ordered his servant, 'Go out quickly into the streets and alleys of the town and bring in the poor, the crippled, the blind, and the lame.'
>
> 'Sir,' the servant said, 'what you ordered has been done, but there is still room.'

Then the master told his servant, 'Go out to the roads and country lanes and make them come in, so that my house will be full. I tell you, not one of those men who were invited will get a taste of my banquet.'"

* * *

Those invited did not attend. One bought a field (a new job); another acquired new oxen (possessions); and someone else got married (human relationship). They prioritized those options and chose not to accept the invitation to the banquet.

The invitation to the banquet is our choice to accept Jesus as our Lord and Savior. We are all invited to the banquet. This is the awareness I believe everyone in their lifetime receives. How many of us refuse to accept God's invitation in favor of our earthly busyness?

We all have earthly commitments, family obligations, jobs, and possessions. We are asked to prioritize Jesus. We are offered the chance, not told, to *accept* God's invitation.

Whether we choose to accept the invitation or not, the banquet still occurs. Those who accept and attend the banquet will celebrate; those who do not accept will continue with their earthly commitments and miss the festivities altogether.

It is not a funeral we are forced to attend; it's a celebration. It is not a famine we are asked to endure; it is a feast we are welcome to enjoy. It's shameful we even question the decision.

The busyness of life can be all-consuming. How does God get someone's attention? This is how God got my mother's awareness, acceptance, and confession. The following testimony is near and dear to my heart. It is my mother's, in her own words.

Mom's Testimony

As a child, I believed in reincarnation. I was taught about reincarnation by my uncle, who lived with my family. He belonged to the Rosicrucian

Order in California. He received literature, which he shared with us. We were fascinated with these religious concepts that we didn't learn in church on Sunday.

He taught us that when we die, we briefly go to heaven to be with God. We are then reborn to experience a new life in a new body, each time evolving until we become as wise and great as Jesus, the great prophet.

We believed Jesus was just a perfect human being, not the Son of God, and we could be like him through many lifetimes of learning. We thought reincarnation was the answer to all of life's questions. For example, someone who plays the piano exceptionally well was probably a great pianist in a previous life. We also had a great philosophy about dying. There was no reason to be sad. Death is only the transition to the next life.

After I married and had children, we regularly attended the local church. I believed in God and reincarnation, and I shared my beliefs with "open-minded" people.

I joined a small women's fellowship group, where we studied Catherine Marshall's book, *Beyond Ourselves*, which talks about giving your life to God, who will give your life a purpose. I said a prayer to give my life to God.

But who was Jesus? For the next six months, I was in complete turmoil over this question. Was Jesus a man or someone to worship? Was God trying to show me Jesus is divine? Some people in our group thought Jesus was real, and you could talk to him!

I invited the group leader to my home to discuss my thoughts. It was a miracle she had the same background as I had! Her father was a Rosicrucian who eventually committed suicide. Her father's beliefs opened the door for Satan.

She was intense. She looked right into my eyes and said, "Reincarnation is *not* of God." We prayed, and she commanded the devil to leave me in the name of the Lord Jesus Christ. I cried so hard. She thanked Jesus for my tears, cleansing me of my past.

That week, every time I thought of the word "reincarnation," the thought burst like a bubble. God did not allow me to even think of the word. That was a second miracle.

Now I love Jesus. Before my conversion, I hated to hear the words "born again" or "savior" or any other words pertaining to salvation. I thought I knew so much more than those born-again Christians. I was completely deceived.

God completely transformed my mind and my heart. He changed my cold, hard heart into a sunbeam for him. God changes us when we give our lives to him and seek his truth. I have been a Christian for over forty years. I was baptized in the Holy Spirit and learned to hear and talk to God.

The group leader who introduced me to Christianity was the last person I ever met who was familiar with Rosicrucianism.

* * *

Thank God for the leader from Mom's church who introduced her to Jesus Christ and ultimately converted her from a believer in reincarnation to a witness for the salvation and passion of Jesus. She, in turn, has saved many people through her testimony.

Because of my mother, I knew from an early age communication with God was possible. I've heard my mother speak in her prayer language. I know she shares a special bond with Jesus. Even today, my mother prays for me and gives me advice based on God's responses. She made me aware, but I did not accept it for myself for many years. I never tried.

STEP 3

SALVATION

† "Mercy triumphs over judgment!" (James 2:13b)

† "Therefore no one will be declared righteous in his [God's] sight by observing the law; rather, through the law we become conscious of sin." (Rom 3:20)

The Old Testament

The Old Testament and the New Testament are separated by Jesus: the old law and the new law, the old way and the new way, BC and AD.

In the Old Testament, sinners suffered for disobeying my commands—physical suffering, death, wars, disasters, floods. Yet despite all the physical evidence of the destructiveness of disobedience, people continued to sin.

If the old law was the foundation for all judgment, the world would be in big trouble. If the commandments were the basis for all judgment, I would not have needed my son Jesus to die on the cross. I can uphold the old law. I sent Jesus to save the world, to save you.

Paul says in Romans 13:9–10 (paraphrased): All the commandments can be summed up in this one rule: love your neighbor as yourself…love is the fulfillment of the law.

These verses describe perfectly the transition from the Old Testament to the New. Jesus provided the love necessary for you to be forgiven from the law.

> ✝ "But if anybody does sin, we have one who speaks to the Father in our defense—Jesus Christ, the Righteous One." (1 John 2:1b)

This passage does not suggest that a willful disregard of the commandments can be overcome by a simple confession. One can't steal from a neighbor, say a quick prayer for forgiveness, and then steal from the other neighbor.

Believing in Jesus does not provide immunity for willful disobedience, but Jesus gives hope for those who have sinned and desire true repentance with the intent of future obedience.

This is the promise provided in the New Testament.

The New Testament

> ✝ "For what the law was powerless to do...God did by sending his own Son in the likeness of sinful man to be a sin offering." (Rom 8:3a)

> ✝ "Therefore, if anyone is in Christ, he is a new creation; the old has gone, the new has come!" (2 Cor 5:17)

> ✝ "Therefore, there is *now* no condemnation for those who are in Christ Jesus, because through Christ Jesus, the law of the Spirit of life set me free from the law of sin and death." (Rom 8:1–2)

> ✝ "For the law was given through Moses; grace and truth came through Jesus Christ." (John 1:17)

Jesus put an end to Old Testament suffering. Jesus suffered for the world, died on the cross, and transformed my job from a disciplinarian into a forgiver. Your belief in Jesus sets you free from eternal suffering.

The commandments are laid out for your guidance, but you cannot uphold them. Humans sin. But through your belief in Jesus and his forgiveness of your sins, you have upheld the law even if you have not lived up to its requirements.

When your world is good, I am. When your world is not so good, I still am. I was, I am, I will be. I am the everlasting, the Almighty, the omnipotent. I am a loving God. I love my children. I am also judgment. I do not tolerate sin. Do not think for one minute that I overlook sin. It is only through my son, who pleads to me on your behalf, that I even consider forgiving your sinful nature. I am the God of the Old Testament—firm, judgmental. Do not put me to the test.

Jesus changed the world for you and for me. Through Jesus, you are able to live within me and I within you through the Holy Spirit. We are able to communicate anytime you want; we no longer need a burning bush or a miraculous transfiguration of the earth.

It is powerful to know all the implications of Jesus's coming, his death, and his resurrection. Only through this deeper understanding do you gain a greater appreciation and love for Jesus.

You have learned the difference between the law, or Old Testament, and the freedom, forgiveness, and salvation of the New Testament. Would I have put my son through such torture if the gains were not great?

Believe and Be Saved!!

† "That if you confess with your mouth, 'Jesus is Lord,' and believe in your heart that God raised him from the dead, you will be saved. For it is with your heart that you believe and are justified, and it is with your mouth that you confess and are saved." (Rom 10:9–10)

Be not concerned with your earthly future, but with your eternal future.

Forgiveness of sins and your salvation are your most important priorities. Of all the steps on your journey, salvation is the ultimate, the only requirement, the key to life and love everlasting. This is what saves lives.

You cannot be forgiven until you recognize and admit to your wrong. Recognizing is much easier than admitting. Next comes confessing, which is admitting to me. Confessing is cleansing; it is the act which cleanses your heart.

You must keep your heart pure. You come to me with a heart in need of cleansing. I will cleanse it, day by day, step by step. I forgive your sins, and I will continue to forgive your sins if you come to me with your heart in your hands and ask for my forgiveness.

† "This righteousness from God comes through faith in Jesus Christ to all who believe." (Rom 3:22a)

There is no such thing as being worthy or unworthy of having fellowship with me. This is Satan's way of discouraging your initiative. It is not through your own deeds you are deemed righteous and worthy, but through your belief in my son Jesus. When you feel unworthy to be in my presence, ask for forgiveness for the reason and move on.

Approach our time together with confidence in your heart, that I delight in your fellowship. Cast aside any doubts or negativity and rejoice. It is your belief and acceptance of Jesus that has opened the door for your salvation and our relationship. This is the only price of admission.

Worthiness is not measured by your acts, but by your heart. I'm looking for desire. You are worthy because you desire to be with me.

Giving me your whole heart is about being centered on me:

> Talk and listen every day
> Pray every day
> Obey every day
> Read the Word every day
> Witness and serve every day
> Love me every day
> Trust me every day
> Love others every day
> Thank me every day

Bring all these actions to me, and you will become whole. At first, you will need to force the habit, then it will become natural and enjoyable.

Who Could Feel Worthy?

My firstborn, my perfect creation, Adam, sinned. He was the first to feel unworthy after the fall of humanity, hiding in the Garden of Eden. It is impossible for humans not to sin.

Who made greater mistakes than David in the Old Testament? He made big mistakes, but it was not out of disrespect for me, or lack of love for me. It was out of human foolishness. David loved me with all his heart. You can feel his love in the Psalms. Love me with all your heart.

Your feelings of unworthiness are not unique. To feel worthy would be irreverent. Be glad you feel unworthy. After you understand and accept your unworthiness, it is no longer a negative, no longer a burden. You can overcome with my grace and move forward to do great work for me.

There is a fine line between being humble and feeling unworthy. Humility opens your mind to learning. The humble recognize their shortcomings and are willing to accept guidance and advice. Staying humble is being grateful in a quiet manner, appreciating what you have been given without boasting, without taking credit for yourself, or drawing attention to yourself.

Only the haughty and proud feel worthy, and they are not. The proud are not receptive. The proud will become disappointed, and the humble will be elevated.

To Those Struggling with Worthiness

Worthiness is not one of my criteria, but it is one of yours. Allow yourself to feel worthy of my love. You continue to open the door for unworthiness. Shut it! This will prevent your growth. You only know earthly worthiness, where everything is earned. This is not so in my kingdom.

Aspects of your personality are greatly affected by this sense of unworthiness, of which you are not aware. For instance, criticism affects you much more than others, because it reinforces your feeling of unworthiness.

This is not something you can fix yourself. You must pray. When you don't ask me for something, it is because you feel you do not deserve it. You deserve it because of your love for me and my love for you! Ask me for greater desires and expect to receive them. Give me the opportunity to demonstrate my love for you. You stifle me by not asking.

Do not feel unworthy because you compare yourself to others. Everyone is at different stages of life, different stages of spirituality. Compare yourself only to where you want to be, where I want you to be, where you feel you should be and could become. Jesus found his disciples in the most unlikely places. You are an angel compared to some of the greatest Christians who ever lived!

Feel worthy of blessing others with your newfound spiritual knowledge. You will feel a greater sense of worthiness when your works develop fruit. This, you will know, is a gift from me.

To Those Struggling with Worthiness — Jesus Inspired

God's grace makes you worthy. Praise be to God for his forgiveness and his love. If worthiness were a criterion for fellowship, God would be lonely.

You can have a wonderful relationship with the God of the universe. Ask him to open doors and shut doors. You need only to walk.

Trust him with your whole heart. Trust he will do what is right.

Would he deny you of works to glorify him? Would he deny you peace and happiness when it is in his power to grant such desires? Would you deny your children?

Pray for his presence to increase throughout your day, every day. Be confident knowing even in your worst days, God is waiting to hear from you.

Strong Foundation

† "Unless the Lord builds the house, its builders labor in vain."
(Ps 127:1a)

Build your spiritual house on a strong foundation of faith. A house built on a strong foundation requires less maintenance during its lifetime than a house built on a shaky foundation. The maintenance necessitated by a weak foundation can be serious; cracked walls, crooked floors, doors that do not properly open and close. These types of repairs generally require professional help to fix.

Foundations are much harder to fix after the house is built. Many people spend their lives performing constant repairs, not recognizing the faulty foundation. Sometimes the house needs to be torn down completely and rebuilt from the ground up.

When building your house, do not rush through the laying of the foundation. Do not be impatient and say, "I want to see what the house is going to look like." The house will be more beautiful and much stronger with a properly constructed foundation.

You build the house, and I'll supply the rock on which to place it. You cannot build the rock, only I can. The rock is your salvation, the starting point for our relationship. I will not let you place a beautiful house on an unstable ledge.

The knowledge that you have built a strong foundation gives you confidence to build the rest of the house. You are gaining knowledge from the lessons learned and confidence that these teachings are from me. As you share these messages, your confidence grows. The more you know about something, the more confident you are to share this knowledge with others.

Many people go through periods of spiritual revival, such as you are experiencing. But many times, the foundation is weak, and the enthusiasm wanes. The urgency disappears, circumstances improve, and I am forgotten. A strong intimate relationship is never formed. The foundation crumbles.

Fix the Leaky Roof

Identify the obstacles in your life that prevent you from maintaining a righteous lifestyle and give them to me. Give me your worries, your sins, your relationships, your past. Tell me what you fear. When you accept my offering and ask for my forgiveness, your life will begin to change. I will reveal and heal your weaknesses. These are like leaks in a roof, which must be identified and repaired.

We will begin to fix your leaky roof. I know why these items control your will, and I'll deal with the cause, not the symptoms. You keep a bucket under the leaky roof because you don't know how to fix it. You fear what might happen if you remove it. Sometimes leaks go away temporarily and then reappear because the source wasn't properly identified.

It may take months to identify the source, and it may take a lifetime of battling to overcome completely. But I will permanently fix the cause of the roof troubles, so you don't have to worry about the leaks (the symptoms) or the buckets (temporary solutions) anymore.

When you accept my grace, your healing will come; it takes time to do it right. Pray for relief/deliverance from these spirits that bind you with these tendencies. They are like diseases, and the blood of Jesus is the medicine.

Whatever bad I filter out of your life will be replaced with good. Your burden will be lighter with the removal of these barriers. You have no control over these issues, no knowledge to fix yourself. Be brave and give them to me. Don't be afraid of losing something you may feel is important because I will replace it with something which is important.

You are the biggest threat to Satan during this period of growth. As we fix your leaks, the outward changes will have people asking questions. This is strong testimony that Satan hates.

These benefits come from accepting my grace and allowing me to lead your life. Your salvation is dependent upon your release of these obstacles, and your ensuing spiritual development awaits.

SALVATION — PERSONAL REFLECTION

If you have not yet asked God for forgiveness and given your life to Jesus, say this prayer out loud with the full faith of your heart:

"Heavenly Father, I come to you in the name of your son, Jesus Christ. I admit I am a sinner, and I confess my sins. I believe with my heart, and I confess with my mouth, Jesus is the Lord and Savior of my life. I believe Jesus died for my sins, and you raised him from the dead. I pray, Lord, for your forgiveness. Thank you, Father God, for saving me and forgiving my sins. I accept my salvation, and I welcome a personal relationship with your son, my Lord and Savior, Jesus Christ. Amen."

* * *

My salvation occurred on Christmas Day 2008 when I broke down in uncontrollable weeping and asked God for his forgiveness. I'm convinced the Holy Spirit prayed this prayer for me. It is written in my journal, but it is much too eloquent for me to take credit for:

"I come to you, Lord, humbled and broken. Hear my prayer, have mercy on me. I confess my sins, O Lord, and ask for your forgiveness.

Cover me with the blood of Jesus, the blood shed on the cross for my deliverance and salvation. I thank you for your grace and mercy, Lord Jesus. I ask for your protection and guidance today. I ask for your peace, love, and joy today. I thank you for the good things in my life and for the good things yet to come. I thank you for your blessings and your forgiveness. I pray, Lord Jesus, that the Holy Spirit guides me and teaches me each and every day. I pray you make it possible for me to do your will."

Old Testament and New Testament

I love the statement, "Jesus turned my job from a disciplinarian into a forgiver." The Old Testament can be brutal. People disobey God, God disciplines the people, the people repent. This cycle repeats itself throughout the Old Testament. Over and over, armies and cities are decimated by fire, floods, famines, and wars. Kings are appointed, kings are killed.

God gave the commandments, but they were continually, repeatedly broken. I'm greatly oversimplifying the Old Testament, but the fact remains God punished sin harshly, in real time, with horrific acts of violence.

God gave the law in the first place to curb human sinfulness, to make clear to humanity what is right and what is wrong. The purpose wasn't punishment. The purpose was to provide a framework for maintaining a righteous relationship with God. Obedience to the law leads to life in fellowship with God. Disobedience leads to death and separation from God.

The Ten Commandments

Jesus taught us to obey God's commandments. In Matt 19:17, Jesus says, "If you want to enter life, obey the commandments." Yet, who of us can even recite the Ten Commandments? Let's paraphrase for a quick refresher:

1. Serve the one and only true God.
2. No idols.
3. Don't use God's name in vain.
4. Keep the Sabbath day holy.
5. Honor your father and mother.
6. Do not murder.
7. Do not commit adultery.
8. No stealing.
9. No lying.
10. Do not envy or obsessively desire another's property.

† "If we claim to be without sin, we deceive ourselves and the truth is not in us." (1 John 1:8)

May the one without sin throw the first stone! These behavioral guidelines inscribed by God form the basis for his judgment. Clearly, no one is throwing any stones!

God is no more tolerant of sin today than he was in the Old Testament. Is our behavior any better today? Why don't *we* experience catastrophic, God-wielded punishment?

Jesus's death and resurrection are the difference. God gave us the opportunity to believe in his son and be forgiven of our sins or suffer the consequences after death. God's role changed dramatically in the New Testament.

This does not mean we can disregard the Ten Commandments if we believe in Jesus. God will not be conned into forgiving the sins of a willful, repeat offender who uses the escape clause to rationalize further sin without consequences. God knows our heart, our level of remorse for our sins, and our sincerity to repent.

Like a parent disciplines a child out of love, God disciplines people out of love. Don't get the wrong idea about God judging and loving people. God loves his people. Whether in the Old Testament or the New Testament, when God punishes people for their sins, the very act is an expression of love. He was not all judgment in the Old Testament and all love in the New Testament. We find in the New Testament, however, that his love took on a new form in Jesus.

The Rock is Our Salvation

God spends a lot of time in these messages talking about construction and how to build a sturdy spiritual house. I also discuss foundations and leaky roofs throughout the text, so I want the meaning to be clear. I'll start from the ground and work my way up to the roof!

God speaks of supplying the rock upon which we can build our foundation. This solid rock, which only God can supply, is salvation. If we desire to build a spiritual house, it must start with God's solid rock of salvation. We cannot create our own salvation. People cannot build rock; only God can grant our salvation.

We build the foundation on top of the rock. The foundation represents the strength of our belief in God, Jesus, and the Holy Spirit. How strong is our foundation of faith? Can it supply the solid footing to support further growth with God? A strong foundation will last a lifetime. A weak foundation will be crushed by the weight of the house. No portion of the foundation can be weak, or the integrity of the house will be jeopardized.

The walls and floors are the relational steps of spiritual maturity. They are built upon our salvation and our unwavering belief in God; the rock and the foundation. As our relationship grows with God through communication, love, trust, obedience, wisdom, and discernment, our spiritual house begins to take shape.

Every one of these spiritual milestones supports each other, like the frame of a house. The house can't have walls without floors. We can't have a complete house with only two or three walls. Fulfillment of purpose is the complete house, walls, floors, and foundation, all built upon the solid rock.

The roof is the human element to the house; our psyche, our self-will, our resolve, our morals. It is the most fragile part, the most likely to be damaged under oppressive circumstances or conditions. The roof protects the house from outside influences. It fights against temptation. It is under attack in all seasons. It is important to maintain an impenetrable barrier to safeguard the rest of the house, for the entire house is at risk if the roof is compromised.

Worthiness in Dad's Eyes

Do you feel unworthy to ask God for salvation? Do you feel like you need to clean up your act before you ask God for forgiveness? What is holding you back?

I never doubted, nor will I ever doubt my dad's love for me. But growing up, it never seemed like anything I did was good enough; at least, to me, it didn't. Honestly, compared to him, it wasn't. He was good at everything. Maybe the tasks he wasn't good at, he never attempted, like cooking. Come to think of it, I never saw him cook anything but eggs.

His work ethic is unbelievable, never-ending. He is creative, mechanically inclined, strong, good at sports, unafraid, street-smart, outgoing. He built a two-car garage behind our house. He can take a car engine apart and put it back together. He can even do his own taxes! He does everything to perfection.

In contrast, as a child, I liked to play. For instance, I invented a dice game that simulated sports. I created one for baseball, football, basketball, even auto racing. I'd play the dice games, most times alone, in my bedroom.

I remember occasions when Dad would be outside working, and he probably needed my help. Maybe he wanted to teach me something. I can recall his disappointment when he came into the house, only to find me playing my childish dice game.

But the fact is, the dice game required me to keep statistics, like baseball box scores, and I enjoyed statistics. I ended up being a CPA and analyzing numbers for a living. I certainly did not know this at the time. I felt like something was wrong with me.

Don't get me wrong, I know my dad loves me more than anything in the world. He was my role model, still is, and I love him very much. But from my child's perspective, he was larger than life, and I was inadequate. I could never compare. I'm certain these childhood experiences created feelings of unworthiness in my little-boy brain that continue to influence my actions today.

Seeking worthiness has always been the biggest driver of behavior for me, probably to a fault. I'm sure this contributed to my workaholism. I seek perfection in everything I do, and I work endlessly in pursuit of excellence. It can be a terrible curse when mediocre would be good enough!

If I could not see myself as worthy in my dad's eyes, how could I ever be acceptable in God's eyes? Who could possibly feel worthy in the presence of God?

I felt constant doubt, unworthiness, and lack of purpose. As a result, worthiness and righteousness seemed all but impossible to achieve, until I received God's message on desire, and the following Bible verses emphasizing the *pursuit* of righteousness:

† "The Lord detests the way of the wicked but he loves those who pursue righteousness." (Prov 15:9)

† "But you, man of God, flee from all this, and pursue righteousness, godliness, faith, love, endurance and gentleness." (1 Tim 6:11)

This discovery is so simple and meaningful. Scripture says to *pursue* righteousness; it does not say we have to *be* righteous! It is the pursuit of the heart that pleases God and brings his blessings. Who can truly attain righteousness? Who can attain worthiness? It is impossible! *But the pursuit is possible for everyone.*

Pursuit indicates diligent effort, not a passing thought. You pursue items you desire with your heart; they dominate your mind and attention.

How perfectly comforting to those of us who are challenged by worthiness! You may feel worthy because of your desire to pursue God. God compares earthly worthiness, where everything is earned through deeds, to heavenly worthiness, defined as the *desire* to be worthy.

Discrimination and Favoritism

† "For God does not show favoritism." (Rom 2:11)

God does not show favoritism, and therefore he does not discriminate. This is a lesson for all who feel inferior in this world, stemming from discrimination, racism, prejudices between languages, religions, countries, and political views.

People are rich, poor, tall, small, fat, and skinny. These factors are irrelevant in God's eyes. He merely asks us to love him with all our heart and to believe in his son Jesus Christ.

The Worthy Centurion

We are not alone in our struggle with worthiness. Refer to the story of the Roman centurion in the book of Luke. He was a man of great worldly accomplishments, certainly worthy in human terms, a man of wealth, a man of authority, and a gentile. He struggled with worthiness as he considered approaching Jesus to heal his sick servant:

> When Jesus had finished saying all this in the hearing of the people, he entered Capernaum. There a centurion's servant, whom his master valued highly, was sick and about to die. The centurion heard of Jesus and sent some elders of the Jews to him, asking him to come and heal his servant. When they came to Jesus, they pleaded earnestly with him, "This man deserves to have you do this, because he loves our nation and has built our synagogue." So Jesus went with them.

He was not far from the house when the centurion sent friends to say to him: "Lord, don't trouble yourself, for I do not deserve to have you come under my roof. That is why I did not even consider myself worthy to come to you. But say the word, and my servant will be healed. For I myself am a man under authority, with soldiers under me. I tell this one, 'Go,' and he goes; and that one, 'Come,' and he comes. I say to my servant, 'Do this,' and he does it."

When Jesus heard this, he was amazed at him and turning to the crowd following him, he said, "I tell you, I have not found such great faith even in Israel." Then the men who had been sent returned to the house and found the servant well. (Luke 7: 1–10)

* * *

We are worthy, not of our own doing but from the grace of God. We are worthy because we allow ourselves to accept God's grace when we ask for and receive salvation.

Foundations and Leaky Roofs

During the transitional period of my life, living at the lake, I quickly discovered the drawbacks of an 1890s–era building. Many features of the house were updated, but the foundation was made of a cobblestone material, which showed its age. Cylindrical steel posts were installed to support the first floor, taking the weight off the tired joists crossing the basement.

This house birthed the concept of the strong foundation and the leaky roof. There were a lot of nice features to the house above the foundation. It was obviously rebuilt and expanded many times over the years, but they could not overcome the faulty foundation.

The water level in my fish tank was noticeably higher on one end than it was on the other side, only two feet away. My pendulum mantel clock, a wedding present given to my grandparents in the 1930s, would not work properly above the fireplace, because I could not find a level surface. Doors stuck, and in some cases, no longer closed. Cracks in the walls and ceiling were common.

Without major repairs to the foundation, this house will always be somewhat of a disaster; beautiful from the outside, messed up on the inside. Eventually, the house will collapse.

How many of us are like this? We have a weak foundation of faith, but we try and build a façade around us to mask our internal struggles. We portray an image of stability and beauty, but the truth will eventually prevail and consume us.

When humans cannot self-diagnose their own issues, they call on professional help from psychiatrists, they rely on friends and neighbors, or perhaps turn to drugs and alcohol, instead of evaluating their own foundation of faith.

Build your house with *God as your foundation*. If you have a crisis later, like a leaky roof, all you need to do is fix the roof, not rebuild the house. Do the only thing you can to solidify your foundation—turn to God.

I love the leaky-roof analogy. Everyone has issues. The easiest short-term solution is to compensate for the leak by placing a bucket to catch the water and minimize the damage. You spend your life moving buckets! What happens to a leaky roof that is not fixed? More leaks develop, more buckets, more attempts to address the symptoms (i.e., by trying drugs and alcohol). Allow God to identify the source, the reason for the leaky roof, and prescribe the best solution to fix it. He will diagnose if you let him.

Your house does not have to be perfect to ask God for salvation. In fact, it is impossible not to have leaks and cracks. Telling God there is a leak isn't news to God.

The act of faith exhibited by asking God for help is the response God is seeking. Don't wait to feel worthy of asking for salvation, because no one is worthy by their own doing. He's willing to help you fix your life, fully aware of the challenges.

Salvation is only step number three on the spiritual ladder. There is plenty of time to fix all the leaks, cracks, and feelings of unworthiness. Prioritize salvation. Pursue God, accept Jesus as your personal savior, and ask God for forgiveness. After you make this commitment, anything is possible with God on your side.

STEP 4

COMMUNICATION

† "Listen, for I have worthy things to say; I open my lips to speak what is right." (Prov 8:6)

THIS CHAPTER CONTAINS A COMPREHENSIVE series of messages from God. Topics range from dedicating time for fellowship to how to journal, forms of communication, overcoming distractions, and feeling the joy that comes with being close to God.

Communication is another milestone Satan will try desperately to prevent. He will fill your head with doubt that communication is possible. You will question whether the voice you hear is from God. It is vital you recognize Satan's attempts to discourage your progress because communication leads to a healthy relationship, deeper love, trust, and obedience. Successful communication creates undeniable proof God exists and makes it easier to realize the other milestones are attainable.

It also opens the door for you to witness. Ultimately, this is a disaster for Satan. Not only are you communicating with God, but you are also communicating with others about God.

* * *

Quiet, Please

Insight: "Rest more with Me. If I, the Son of God, needed these times of quiet communion with My Father, away, alone, from noise, from activity—then surely you need them too."[1]

I wrote my first message from God sitting in the man chair in my living room on January 6, 2009. However, most of my quiet time took place in my bedroom, either early in the morning before work or late at night before bed.

I made the bed to avoid any temptation to crawl in and gathered my materials—writing journals, the Bible, my favorite pen, and other books I might be reading, including the *Daily Guideposts* devotional.

It is critical to remove the temptation of telephones and mobile devices—all possible distractions which could interfere with complete dedication and concentration.

Find a place comfortable for you, which is conducive to relaxation. For me, the lake view from my rental home provided a peaceful setting; its beauty supplied endless inspiration. A beautiful view is not necessary, it just happened to be a bonus for me.

When I am ready to approach God, I write the date at the top of the page in my journal, and I sit quietly. Writing the date gets the ink flowing, which, to me, symbolizes the flow of communication. I have never marked the date in my journal and written nothing. It has become a sign of trust and faith. I write the date because I expect to hear from God. I know it; God knows it. I should expect to hear from him.

I boldly state the following out loud, "I close the door of my heart, my mind, and my spirit to everything except the word of God." This sets the stage for me. I am intentionally dedicating this time to God!

Then I rest and allow myself to enter a deep calm. Athletes speak of getting into the zone, a state of consciousness that transcends normal participation in an activity. The participants become so consumed in the performance that they become oblivious to crowd noise, pain, game pressure, and nerves.

I refuse to use the word "meditation" to describe this feeling of peace. To me, meditation implies a mindless consciousness, a brain devoid of all thoughts. When I seek communion with God, my mind is focused on God and oblivious to all other thoughts. I search for God as if I am reaching out to him with my mind, concentrating solely on finding him, waiting for him to connect.

If I want conversation, I'll be quiet to hear the thoughts God places in my mind. I've learned not to doubt my faith or become impatient when I do not receive an immediate response. I have knocked on the door to communication, and I know God will answer.

I may feel the inclination to pray, or open my Bible and read a few verses, or maybe open my journal and jot down some thoughts. Some mornings I start writing instantly like there's something pressing God wants to tell me. God may invite me to verbally ask or write down questions to initiate the conversation. I follow whatever urges I sense. If it does not feel satisfying, I settle down and allow myself to feel nudged in a different direction.

I always recognize his voice, regardless of the source of inspiration, as my spirit comes to life. I've discovered books and music complement my experiences and become a regular part of my communication and celebration with God. But the focus should always be on God. Everything else should facilitate communication with God.

In the beginning, I had to be completely comfortable and alone, so I would not worry about possible interruptions. I did not even attempt to communicate with God if anyone was in the house. Otherwise, I would expectantly lie there and wait for a knock on the door. It was simply too distracting. I needed to be totally committed to this time with God and God alone.

The need for isolation dissipated with time. Eventually, it became easier to get into this mental zone and even remain in the zone amidst distractions. After you experience God's peace and your mind knows how it feels, you can achieve this state of mind without the solitude, allowing you to feel it at anytime, anywhere. I've written messages in public places surrounded by all kinds of activity, mentally focusing and spiritually tuning my heart to hear from God.

This segment of time is the most important part of my day. I look forward to it. I enjoy it. The joy and peace carry me through the rest of the day. I don't want to start my day without it! My demeanor is noticeably better on days when I dedicate time to God, and noticeably worse when I don't. If you have trouble carving out time in your day, pray for God to help you find time, and he will. If you have trouble finding a quiet place, buy earplugs!

Taking time to be with God always calms me down. Whether I spend thirty minutes, forty-five minutes, or an hour, it always seems to end prematurely. I run out of time, wishing I could stay longer in God's presence.

COMMUNICATION— INSPIRATION FROM GOD

Daily

People have become more independent, self-willed, driven by earthly gatherings, and less dependent on me. They come to me when it is convenient or when they are in need. I listen, and I welcome those moments. There is a core of belief, of hope, but it is not lasting. People cannot feel the full extent of my love once a week, or once a month. I yearn for a daily, hourly relationship.

Be persistent in finding time for me every day. Begin each day by acknowledging and appreciating my presence. Find time for me when you have a stressful day ahead. You say, "I am too stressed!" Come to me with your troubles. Break your habit of diving into the day's busyness unarmed. Evenings may be more peaceful than your mornings. The day is over. There is no urgency to hurry to work; you can relax easier. Better yet, make time in the morning and evening!

There is no substitute for spending time directly with me. You have accepted my gift of hearing and learning, so continue to develop this spiritual awareness. Meditate on my Word, pray, it doesn't matter. Take the time to be with me in spirit. Your desire to spend time in quiet devotion is evidence of my indwelling. Otherwise, you would not make the time or miss the time.

Charge your spirit every day, or it will lose its power, like a battery. You have no dead cells in your battery; your spirit receives the charge quickly. It is full of life, as you are. When your spirit is charged, you are more energized and vibrant!

Quiet-Time Advice—Jesus Inspired

If you can't sense God's presence, just relax and pray. Let the Holy Spirit guide you. Do not ritualize this time with a preset agenda, for God may want to take you in a different direction.

When God wants your attention, he will get it. If God wants to say something to you, he will, as long as you give him the opportunity. God delights in the time you have made for him. He knows you are expectant. Expect the same from him.

Giving God time every morning demonstrates your faith and desire despite your lack of understanding. It is not possible for you to understand, only for you to have faith. Therefore, you can only do what you are capable of doing and let God do the rest.

Do not substitute works during this time set aside for God. Without his guidance, your works will become misguided and, eventually, meaningless.

Every day will make you stronger, will make you complete. You have a choice. Choose every day.

Schedule the Time!

Your time is not limited. You limit your time, which limits your learning. Take time for me; not the minimum time but the available time.

You say your schedule is too busy? Spending a short period of time together is all it takes to break the momentum of busyness. Put me on your schedule! You have a choice. Choose to spend time with me. I will make time in your day if your will is to spend it with me. What could be more important than spending time with the God of the universe!

Prioritize the actions of your life. To "not have time" simply means you did not make time. What factors dictate your priorities? How do you determine what you do today, versus what you do tomorrow? Prioritize me!

Do not overburden yourself because of others. The people you think need you, need you less than you think. Place me before everything else and everyone else.

I know your desires, I know your anxieties, I know your impatience, I know your obstacles. I know what I am doing. Trust me, and give me this time, and you will not miss a thing.

Sometimes the point is simply to give you peace. I may ask you to sit silently before me, and I may speak no words you could write. Wait with me so I can bring comfort. Only friends who understand and love each other are comfortable waiting silently in each other's presence. I may prove our friendship by asking you to wait in silence while I rest with you.

Dedicate the Time

Don't set time aside and then play with your computer. Turn off the gadgets. Do not let anything interfere with this time. Make up your mind to dedicate an hour, and then don't think about anything else until the hour is over.

Do not focus on today's to-do list; doing the laundry, taking out the garbage, emptying the dishwasher, and thinking of your schedule at work. This is not what I mean by dedicating time to me. This is fitting me in between washing the sheets and doing the dishes as if I am one more chore. Concentrate on nothing but me. You will find time to get these chores done.

You have too many distractions? I am the God of the universe. How many distractions do you think I have? Yet I am always available when you call on me!

Ask me to block out your distractions. Concentrate on me, and your thoughts will not be scattered. These distractions are your own free will exercising dominance over your willingness to be silent and obedient. Be sincere about closing the door to these distractions, so your mind may be purposeful and dedicated to me.

Do not read someone else's book on my time. I would rather spend the time with you. Save the other books for the nightstand. Dedicate the time to me, and as excess time permits, do your supplemental readings and research. Do not discard them, for they may create opportunities to corroborate messages.

Put yourself in a position of complete commitment and concentration. Do something physical, like getting on your knees, which tells your mind and body it is my time; time to spend with your Lord and Savior, and you are not to be bothered!

Be with me, solely. How do you feel when you want to talk to someone, and they won't stop to listen to you? They continue to do other activities and give you the "uh-huh." You would consider it disrespectful. Don't be disrespectful with me.

When you work on a big project at the office, you enter a deep level of concentration. No interruptions and no distractions! Am I not more important than a spreadsheet or a PowerPoint? You have developed the discipline to find time for me, now find the discipline to dedicate the time completely to me.

The World Will Not Slow Down for You

Just say no. Your busyness is not a healthy activity. Satan knows you cannot say "no" to an activity. The flood of events in your life is causing unnecessary stress. Unnecessary because they are voluntary, social stresses from activities you choose above and beyond the normal life and work stresses.

Your week ahead is full of work commitments, full of after-work commitments. Take time for yourself before it is too late. Your inconsistency in finding quiet time only hurts you. Slow down your pace of life and occasionally say no, because the world will not slow down for you.

Defeat Life's Whirlwind

You hear the cars and trucks speeding by the house. This is the busyness of life. You delight in the sanctity of our fellowship, but shortly you will be one of them, absorbed by the whirlwind of your busy life. Hear the sounds of the world and take comfort in me.

Your job makes you anxious. How do you keep up the pace? The intensity? The long hours? Do not get sidetracked by these distractions. Life's worries and anxieties disappear during your period with the Spirit. It takes practice to ignore the outside world, but when our channel of communication is clear, anything is possible.

Feel my peace in the busyness, amidst every imaginable distraction. I am with you always.

Live in Me All Day

Dedicated time is extremely important—every day—but the rest of the day can be ours together as well. I enjoy what you enjoy. I can be with you while you work on your car, while you work on house projects. I will also help you when you are doing activities you don't enjoy.

Rejoice during your commute; rejoice during your day. Let's spend the day together. Put your day in my hands. Sometimes the simplest daily activities create opportunities for us to grow closer together. You must learn this, or you will miss out on one of the greatest benefits of our relationship.

Pause during the day. Feel my presence outdoors; my touch in the breeze; my power in the tall, strong trees; my calm on the lake. It is easier to find peace when you are surrounded by my beauty.

To Journal...

You demonstrate your faith every day when you open your journal, write the date at the top of the page, and anticipate receiving some direction. Not a single day do you not hear from me, even under some of the toughest circumstances.

You tend to hear better when you write and to understand better when you reread later. So, always be prepared to write. This could be your ready signal; your quiet place is the pad of paper and pen and not a physical location. Start writing your own thoughts and get the ink flowing. Before you know it, your writing is not your own.

Buy another journal to write down personal messages, lessons just for you and not for sharing with others. You only write lessons you are comfortable sharing, but I have much to teach about you too!

A prayer book is also a good idea. Write your prayers every day. You will see them answered. It may not always be, "Okay, I'll do that now," but you will look back and know I heard you.

Whenever you feel lost, distant from me, reread your notes for reassurance I am with you. These are your own Bible stories, personalized to your life.

...Or Not to Journal

You don't need to write in your journal every day. Reading and writing are important, but quiet time with me is irreplaceable. Do not be consumed by the writing. Be consumed in me. The next page of your journal is still the next page, regardless of the date at the top! Do not burden this time with an obligation to write something. No one is keeping track.

Would you want your children to bring a pad and pen every time they come to you? If there is something you learn or want to remember, then write it. Otherwise, relax in my presence, and cap the pen!

Periods of Absence

† "The Lord is with you when you are with him. If you seek him, he will be found by you, but if you forsake him, he will forsake you." (2 Chr 15:2)

I know everything about you. I know when you are avoiding me, but this does not void me. Instead, approach me with your acknowledgment of sins, and allow me to forgive your shame, so you no longer feel the need to avoid. How would you feel if you had done nothing wrong, yet you were ignored by someone you love?

By counting the number of entries in your journals, you realize you come to me less often than you thought. Lately, the frequency has lessened. Is it any wonder you feel distanced? You have distanced yourself, not I.

Prove to me you can be consistent. How can I task you with something if I cannot be sure you will complete it? I know your desire is sincere, but your worldly commitments often overshadow our time together.

When you continue to give me the time and don't get inspired, how do you feel? Is this a dry time? Do you give up? Do you think I need to warm up to you, and you to me, after a couple days of absence? Do you not know me by now? Do you think I do not know you? Have I not been with you the whole time? Do you think I am only with you during our mornings together?

If you do not expect to hear from me for any of those reasons, you probably won't. When you are absent from me, you will feel absent, but know you are not.

Forms of Communication

There are many sources of communication and inspiration. I speak in many ways—through the Bible, through others, to your listening ears, and through convictions in your heart. If you can't hear, open your Bible and listen. One way is not better than another!

Don't focus solely on one form of communication while ignoring the other sources. Many people miss me entirely because they are too narrow-minded. They have a preconceived idea regarding how communication should occur and are not receptive to alternate channels. Every form of communication can be equally powerful.

Your awareness of my presence in this world, in whatever form or fashion, is evidence of my presence within you.

COMMUNICATION — PERSONAL REFLECTION

EXPECTATION IS AN OVERRIDING CHALLENGE to communication. If you are not receptive, you will not receive.

I hear my mother pray in her prayer language. She is convinced this gift is available to everyone. We pray together for my prayer language. I try on my own to utter the same sounds I hear from my mother's lips, but I don't feel anything supernatural. I believe it is possible, but I honestly am not *expecting* it right now. I know when I'm genuinely ready, I will be able to receive this blessing God offers.

Expectation is not something you can fake. You must believe it is possible with your heart, not your brain. I'm trying my best to convince you that communication with God is possible, but ultimately you must believe. You may have already heard God's voice and did not recognize him. Be patient, be persistent, be expectant. God speaks in a still, small voice.

> † "Then a great and powerful wind tore the mountains apart and shattered the rocks before the Lord, but the Lord was not in the wind. After the wind there was an earthquake, but the Lord was not in the earthquake. After the earthquake came a fire, but the Lord was not in the fire. And after the fire came a gentle whisper." (1 Kgs 19:11b–12)

I cannot overemphasize the importance of finding time every day to be with God if you want to develop a relationship with him. Communication will not happen without dedicating quiet time for the sole purpose of connecting with him.

Find time *today*! Right now, if you can! Worry about tomorrow, next week, next month when the time arrives. The Lord's Prayer says, "Give us *this day* our *daily* bread." Jesus taught us to pray for today first. God will give us today what we need today.

It's Time to Try

If you are in a quiet place right now, put this book down and close your eyes, clear your head of all distractions, and be still. Find a pen and paper. This may be the day that changes your life forever. Pray this prayer with your heart:

"Father God, I praise you, Lord, and thank you for all my blessings. For all I have that is good, I thank you and praise you. I pray, Lord, for your forgiveness of my sins. I pray for you to cleanse my heart and cover me with the blood of Jesus. I desire a deeper relationship with you, Father God. Please allow me to be still, Lord. Please allow me to hear your still, small voice. Please allow me to be aware of your presence. I pray this in the name of your son, Jesus Christ, Amen."

Close your eyes, remain still, be prepared to write whatever you are thinking, especially if it begins with, "I love you, my child." Respond with your thoughts and see where it goes! It could literally be the beginning of a conversation with God.

Be patient. Continue to relax and clear your mind. Pray silently. Ask God to reveal himself. Allow yourself to slip into a state of complete calm. This could take a couple of minutes, five minutes, twenty minutes—don't give up. Don't let your mind wander. You will know when you reach this place of peace.

Do not be afraid to write everything which comes into your mind, even if you think they are your own thoughts. Don't filter through them at this time. Writing your own thoughts may be purposeful! Write freely, without reservation. You are being obedient by innocently opening up to God. You can make sense of your notes and punctuation later.

If you get impatient, stay in the moment and write about the experience in your journal. Start a conversation with yourself and see if God chimes in.

If you have a distraction that keeps you from complete concentration, get rid of it. Stop the clock pendulum, close the curtains, get more comfortable, find a warm blanket, or do whatever it takes to find complete peace.

Most importantly, expect something to happen. Anything. The slightest thought, maybe a small coincidence, will catch your attention, increase your confidence, and provide a building block for tomorrow. Continue to pursue God daily with this level of commitment, and you will find each other.

Busy-ness! Busy-ness!

Insight: "Busy-ness! Busy-ness! You are spreading yourself too thin to avoid looking at Me and doing what I want you to do. You have heard My call clearly. Your scatteredness is a deliberate weapon of Satan who would defeat Me in you. He loves to spread people. Center in Me."[2]

It's not easy to find time for God. We are all busy. There is no age discrimination, and it cuts across race and gender. Everyone has issues. The following are examples from different days in my journal expressing my struggles, prayers, and questions.

* * *

Making time during our busy lives is difficult. Every day is challenging, and sometimes it seems impossible to pause. I have too much on my mind. I look back, and five days have passed. Why is daily prayer so challenging to schedule?

(Prayer) "I need a period of quiet; maybe before I fall asleep, maybe during the day while driving, maybe a combination of all these throughout the day. Show me, Lord, how to find time every day to be with you. I do a lousy job on my own."

* * *

During our periods of silence, is it really God who abandons us or do we abandon God? God never left me. I did not make the time for him. I feel the doors opening to a more personal relationship with God.

(Prayer) "Father, I know you are with me all the time. It is I who chooses not to be with you. I get too busy, and I choose to ignore you. Thank you for this awareness. Thank you for welcoming me back. It was *my* absence and *my* decision to be away. I thank you for the desire to spend time with you, Lord. I thank you for bringing me back, for sharing with me, for helping me grow."

* * *

(Prayer) "The world is full of pressures; time pressures, societal pressures, and economic pressures. I need to slow down and take time for you, Lord. I failed the last two months to find time to be with you despite knowing how wonderful it can be!"

How rare it must be for people to get started on this journey when they have not yet realized the beauty of what lies ahead. How many people are just plain unaware? How do you get people to begin this adventure without making the mistakes and sacrifices I made?

Peaks and Valleys — God Inspired

The view is so beautiful and the feeling so good from the top of the mountain. But it cannot last, because the sustenance is in the valley. Eat of the fruit of the valley and enjoy the peaks of the mountains. Both serve a purpose. Both offer rewards. Do not forsake one to gorge on the other.

* * *

You will experience many highs and lows, peaks and valleys—times when communication flows easily, and disturbing periods of silence. There are mountaintops and valleys. In all situations of silence, look at yourself to find the answers. Do not blame God. He is waiting for you. Pray for his guidance through the valleys, and he will lead you.

I have included some personal peaks and valleys, so you can sense the overwhelming joy of the peaks and the emptiness of the valleys. You may find it humorous. God says both serve a purpose, but the peaks (the highs) are obviously much better than the valleys (the lows). Maybe the valleys make the peaks seem even higher!

(Peak) I woke up this morning to a colorful, peaceful sunrise and a beautiful inner glow; a spiritual outpouring of praise and thanksgiving. I raised my hands, and an unusual tingling sensation flowed through my body. I have peace despite the chaos of my personal life; the probability of divorce, the stress from moving again, changes in my responsibilities at work.

(Peak Prayer) "You know the desires of my heart and the fears in my head. I delight in you, Heavenly Father. I revere this time together above all else. It is wonderful. I am so thankful, Heavenly Father, for where I am today. I have found myself, and I have found you."

(Valley) When I hear nothing, I feel like I'm doing something wrong. Doubts surface about ever hearing from God again. I don't understand the periods of silence. I feel comfort and peace, but I don't feel accomplished, like I've wasted my time.

(Peak) Walking in the park brings me closer to Jesus. It is easier to feel his presence, freer than the solitude of my bedroom or hotel room. The solitude is more formal, but nature is friendlier.

(Valley) Meetings, travel, stressful days at work, gloomy weather, uncertainties, all contribute to a lack of inspiration and motivation. Lately, it seems the peaks and valleys are closer together, almost daily. I feel like I am on a spiritual roller coaster. Some days I am flying high, filled with the Holy Spirit, feeling privileged, blessed, close to God. Today I don't.

(Peak) It's Sunday morning, and I woke up early to spend extra time in devotion before going to church. I have no time pressure. I'm relaxed and comfortable. I have done well to find quiet time when possible, but this allotted time always has limits. I've given Jesus a time slot and deadline. Well, I don't like having time constraints. I like what I am feeling now, no time limit!

(Valley) I have gone four days without writing in my journal. I went to church yesterday. I read a lot. But I have no entries. Lord, I have been learning, but I have not *been* with you.

(Peak) Today's weather is the epitome of a Rochester, New York, winter. The landscape is tree-bark brown, the ground is white, and the sky is different shades of gray. The lake is black. No color in sight. No sign of a sunrise. Looks like it's twenty degrees outside, or worse!

Inside, I am listening to my stereo, praising God, and celebrating. A party of one! Surrounded by my books, journals, and CDs, and I have an hour and a half to enjoy!

Thank you for showing me this beauty during an otherwise cold, wintry, blustery morning. Good morning, Jesus!

(Valley) Am I all out of lessons? This is a period of silence. Why am I experiencing this silence? Let's figure out why! I don't feel far from God, but I don't hear him. I can find some peace, but not completely. I feel at fault, but still wish God could work his way through my clutter to reach me. Especially now, when he knows I am questioning his absence!

I must not doubt God during these quiet periods, during the down moments. Isn't God waiting with open arms when I go back and seek him again? When I really want God, isn't he always there?

(Peak and Valley) This morning I got up at five and walked to the lake. The first time in eighteen months I went down to my dock to see the sunrise and enjoy God's presence. Maybe sometimes you must put yourself out there and let God come to you. It was a wonderful feeling of freedom and beauty and closeness with God's great creation.

Then it rained.

* * *

Clearly, these euphoric moments were precious when my emotional state was good, and I fully engaged with the Holy Spirit and enjoyed my fellowship with God.

But what about the valleys? When my emotional state was not so favorable, and I was unable to get the spiritual high, who did I blame? Many times, I would view this as a spiritual drought. I would blame God for ignoring me or question whether I had done something to make God mad at me. I did not realize the valleys also serve a purpose.

My spiritual enthusiasm was often tied to my feelings, which was not fair to God. God does not have peaks and valleys; only we have peaks and valleys. Our connection with God should not be tied to our mood. What if God approached us in the same manner? God feels bad one morning, so he decides to punish us. God feels offended when we have not paid enough attention to him, so he gives us the cold shoulder! No, this is not how it works.

We all have peaks and valleys, both emotionally and spiritually. The question is, how do we overcome this turbulence to maintain a consistent, healthy relationship with God? Or more specifically, how do we deal with the valleys?

Valleys occur. This cannot be avoided. Life happens, and it's not always great. Depression, anger, pain, helplessness, sorrow, anxiety, and busyness are all real obstacles that hurt healthy relationships. How patient are we with spouses and children when we are experiencing these feelings? It is difficult!

Our friends and family may recognize our state of mind, but God knows exactly how we feel and why. He is within us! With this recognition, I suggest the following advice to prevent your life's valleys from interfering with your spiritual development:

1. Do not enter your time of fellowship with doubt. If you let your life's valleys create doubt that you will connect with God, then it won't happen. Know he longs for you to seek him with anticipation and expectation, not doubt.
2. Pray for relief from the depression caused by your life circumstance. God has the most wonderful ways of making us feel better in our worst moments. He has much better remedies than we could ever design.
3. Be open and optimistic about God's ability to help. God will provide solutions. They may not be your solutions, but one thing is for sure; he will not join the pity party!
4. Seeking God when life isn't going so well is the best opportunity for us to witness his presence, grace, and power. Instead of allowing your emotions to destroy your spiritual well-being, allow your spiritual strength to improve your personal attitude and circumstances.

Quiet Time at the Park

I am certain as you grow closer to God, you become a greater target for Satan. Distractions increase, pressures build, schedules fill up. It will be harder to find devotional time, read the Bible, and pray. You may have experienced opposition while reading this book! Satan will throw whatever he can at you to disrupt your fellowship with God. Here is an example from my notes one cool fall morning early in my journey.

* * *

I am alone and out of town, not an unfamiliar scene for me. It is usually easy to settle down before work and spend time with God because there are fewer morning obligations when I am traveling.

Today, I'm overwhelmed with distractions. I am not able to mentally rest. I can't seem to concentrate on prayer or get into the devotion zone.

I have a cold and don't feel well. I have work deadlines and a long to-do list. Winter is coming. The apartment upstairs sounds like it's being renovated. The traffic outside seems to be all loud trucks, and now I hear every little noise inside and outside the apartment! It's amazing how many distractions you can have *when you're alone!*

I decide to leave, take all my gear, and go to the nearby park. This should work. How distracting can a park be at seven on a weekday morning?

I position my car facing a beautiful pond with a water fountain. I attempt to find my quiet time in the car, with the journal on the dash and my books on the passenger seat.

Too cramped.

I spot a picnic table overlooking the pond. Perfect! I move to the picnic table. This is all going to work out great! Well, I must be onto something powerful, because the distractions only increase.

First comes the spider, right up onto my journal. Then the city maintenance truck parks on the grass between me and my scenic pond to empty the trash containers. Now there are ants in my coffee! How much trash can there be? Is the garbage truck ever going to move? Where did that spider go? This is not working out as planned!

Then the breeze picked up and turned my journal pages to the following:

> Sometimes when distractions are many, it is because the opposition has intensified. Committing yourself to me will draw increased attention from the evil one and his powerful demons. Be prepared. Understand this

phenomenon and know that Satan has no power or authority over you, as long as you are with me.

The distractions have been designed by the evil one to discourage you from seeking me. As expected, they have multiplied since our relationship evolved. The evil one has lost his grip and is grasping. You feel you have accomplished nothing, but you have been resisting temptations.

You drove to a public park in the city to find solitude. What a change! What a great feeling to experience our fellowship in this unusual setting, a far cry from the sanctity of your quiet room. As you grow in your development in solitude, so, too, will you learn to fellowship anywhere, anytime. When you find time for me outside of your normal setting, stay there until you feel comfort and peace with me, and this, too, shall become your domain. Close your eyes, and the distractions will be greatly reduced.

Conquer this, and you can conquer all.

Don't Force It!

Insight: "To the listening ear I speak, to the waiting heart I come. Sometimes, I may not speak. I may ask you merely to wait in My Presence, to know that I am with you.

Comfort Me, a while, by letting Me know that you would seek Me just to dwell in My Presence, to be near Me, not even for teaching, not for material gain, not even for a message—but for Me." ³

At the end of November 2009, I noticed a decline in the number of journal entries (another benefit of the journal is recognizing your level of time commitment). My entries were no longer daily; they were more infrequent. I was disappointed in my current valley and vowed to write in my journal every day during the month of December.

Unfortunately, I discovered that forcing myself to write every day became a burden, and I lost the joy of quiet time. I lost the flexibility of listening to music and praising God, celebrating and relaxing in his presence because I was too intent on journaling! My quiet time had become homework, a daily chore.

On December 16, I wrote the following:

Every day I feel compelled to write something in this journal to prove I can do it. And I will continue to do it every day because I said I would. But I am realizing, about halfway through this month, the self-imposed necessity to write has removed the joy. The time has become too structured, too predictable, and too forced.

There is no question the time set aside should be for loving, peaceful communion, not a forced obligation. God does not want this time to be a burden. We would not want our children to spend time with us out of a sense of duty when they really want to do something else! God wants to enjoy time with us, as we would with our children.

* * *

One of those December Sundays, I dedicated the entire day to God. It was another dreary Rochester day, and I was alone. I was determined to take my relationship with God to another level. I spent the entire day reading the Bible, trying to experience something new, forcing myself to forego all activity that wasn't spiritual. I confined myself to the bedroom, then to the recliner in the family room, trying to find the perfect spot, the perfect Bible verse, the perfect message. It was a disaster. I completely wasted the entire day and was extremely disappointed and frustrated. I did not enjoy myself at all.

On Monday, God revealed my day could have been spent tinkering with my car, listening to Christian music, doing anything I enjoy while fellowshipping with him. It was a good lesson for me. This is how I can stay with Jesus all day. I had all the right intentions, but I became too inflexible and narrow-minded.

Don't make our relationship too complicated. Allow yourself to celebrate. Yesterday, you put too much pressure on yourself to "put in a good day with God."

Wish you could do yesterday over? It could have been a much better day. You were in complete control over your day's agenda, and you ruined it!

Something as simple as playing your favorite music would have relaxed you. Instead, you tried too hard to dedicate your day to me in a structured way, not in your way!

This lesson could not have been learned until you were by yourself; otherwise you would have excuses for your distractions and dissatisfaction. You will not need to learn this lesson again, so do not be afraid to spend time alone. This is one of the best parts of the Christian life that most people miss out on—living in the Spirit. Living! You certainly did not live yesterday.

* * *

I also learned a lesson from a loving father's perspective. It would be tragic to walk into your child's bathroom and see a sticky note attached to the bathroom mirror with the words "Talk to Dad today."

God knew my thoughts. He knew I had a virtual note on my bathroom mirror. I took the joy out of our relationship that month by forcing communication.

* * *

† "God speaks in different ways, and we don't always recognize his voice." (Job 33:14 CEV)

Later in the month, I was not feeling the connection. I was prepared to have my morning quiet time, but nothing happened. I could have forced myself to continue trying, stubborn in my conviction to write something, and repeated the mistake I made earlier in the month.

Instead, I played a Christian rock CD and heard the most perfect lyrics. I listened to the CD and relaxed, sang along, and had a wonderful bonding experience with God. I would have missed a beautiful experience if I had tried to follow a morning ritual instead of simply enjoying the beauty of music and worship.

* * *

Today you have found peace surrounded by music. It is not necessary to be quiet to receive peace and comfort. Great music stretches the soul and gives the spirit room to grow. As powerful as words can be, when put to beautiful music, the blessings are amplified! Alleluia. Rejoice in this freedom, in this beauty; this is a joy of life. Enjoy the gift of music.

Insight: "When you are tense, full of the burdens of those around you, the problems of your home, look at or listen to something beautiful, and rest will come into your body, mind, and spirit. Make it a deliberate intent, when burdened, to let some of My beauty of which the world is full, enlarge you, relax and strengthen you." [4]

Stay with Jesus All Day

God scolded me recently. I have not found time for him since I began typing this manuscript. I have been working diligently for an hour or two a day, doing God's work, but I am not dedicating the hour of quiet time to be alone with God. I am too busy again.

God revealed I was missing the point. The purpose is not to commune with him for an hour in the morning but to live with him all day.

Christians I admire live with Christ all day. They are overly joyous, friendly, and helpful. I'm sure you know the type of person I am talking about! I may have been skeptical as to their genuineness. I now know this may be the answer! I want that! Being with God all day is my new spiritual goal.

Maybe my next book will describe how I learned to live with God all day. For now, I bought a wristband to wear. It is black with a white cross and quotes Philippians 4:13: "I can do all things through Christ," to remind me what is really important, all the time. I'm sure this wristband is not going to transform me into one of those model Christians, but if it makes me a better person incrementally, then it's a good start. I suspect this is going to be another one of those desires only God can satisfy as we continue down this journey together.

You don't need to talk to Jesus to be in his presence. Do not put all the pressure on the communication. You can delight and take comfort in his presence anytime, anywhere. Walk in a park, have a beautiful walk with Jesus. Bare your soul to him. He will hear.

Reflection on Year One

Christmas of 2009 marked the one-year anniversary of my cleansing, the day I spent weeping, the day I discovered God. I realized how far I had developed spiritually in my first year, how powerful and important the time with God had become in my life.

I saw a difference in others I was close to, ways God touched them through me. God made me brave, independent, and confident in our relationship. In his presence, I cried, I laughed, I was amazed.

Curiosity inspired me to read more. I listened to Christian talk radio and sermons. I volunteered at church. I shared my experiences. I read books about Jesus, which gave me added insight into his life on earth.

I acquired the knowledge and the material from which to build upon spiritually; the discipline, the desire. I communicated freely. I focused my petitions to become closer to Jesus on a personal level and to accept his personal guidance.

I had no idea how much of the journey was still to come! I was enjoying the current ride, this newfound information superhighway God created to fill my journals.

I was a completely transformed spiritual person, with a sense of momentum driving me to grow deeper and deeper in my relationship with God.

STEP 5

RELATIONSHIP

We Are Alike, You and I

Our relationship can easily be explained. You were created in my likeness, so we share the same emotions. Certainly, I am aware of yours. I am the Father, you are my child. This phrase is commonly spoken but not taken to heart. This is a big disconnect. When you are happy, I am happy. When you are stressed, I feel your stress. All you feel, I feel also. All you want, I want for you.

Relationship Growth

How do you judge the strength of a relationship? The ability to talk freely about anything? Comfort in each other's presence? Absence of conflict, no threat of confrontation? Knowledge of each other's likes and dislikes? Mutual respect? The ability to catch up quickly after an absence? The ability to be apart and still feel connected?

Family and a few friends may meet these criteria, but what about Jesus? Can't these same attributes be used to define a relationship with him?

* * *

God as a Father

Compare my role as the Father to your feelings as a parent. When you understand this kind of love, you are better at receiving it. When you receive it, you can give it. I am the Father who feels for you as you feel for others.

I am not a million miles away. Do not say, "Please be with me, Father," for I am there. Do say, "Please let me feel your presence, Father; let me feel your love, your mercy, your grace. Please give me comfort by letting me know you are here. Let me feel your guiding hand, your gentle touch."

You must desire this relationship; I cannot force my intimacy onto you. It is a choice you make. I will be the Father you want me to be. I will be close if you want me close. I will be distant if you push me away. People say they want to be close to me, but their actions and dedication say otherwise.

I am thrilled when a child of mine comes to me without his own agenda and asks if he can help, knowing I will consider his capabilities and assign an appropriate task as you would for one of your children. Would you ask one of your children to do something you knew they were not capable of doing? What purpose would this serve?

As a parent, you have watched your child attempt new things, withholding your involvement so the child will learn, assisting so the child will succeed. One without the other is not good parenting. I know when you are struggling, and I will not let you fail.

If your child displays great effort with a task, are you not inclined to help him? Is not your contribution greater because you want him to complete the task successfully, and you want to show your appreciation for his effort? After all, sometimes success or failure is inconsequential; it is the effort and the bonding experience that is important.

Now let's take this a step further. What if your child puts forth a tremendous effort to do something for you? Unselfishly! Without being asked! Only because he loves you and wants to show his appreciation. How wonderful the feeling for both of you!

You can relate because you were raised in a loving family. You understand the concept of love and the feeling of intimacy, guidance, and protection. There are many who do not know this feeling and cannot relate.

When your children are silent, how badly do you wish you knew what they were thinking? Why? So you could help them! You would do everything possible to abate those fears. Most teenagers keep those feelings inside. How much better would you be as a parent if you knew your child's innermost fears? I know your innermost fears and desires.

Do not come to me under a sense of obligation. What happens when you perform a task out of obligation rather than desire? There is no enthusiasm! I want enthusiasm! I want the child who wants me! Come to me with joy, with anticipation and excitement.

How to Fear and Love—Jesus Inspired

Our Father is a loving Father. He is the Almighty God. It is not God of the universe and son, it is Father and son.

Fear God out of respect for his power, but do not be afraid of him. He sent me to show the world his love for you. Through me you have no reason to fear him. Through me you will feel his love and be protected by his power.

You seek and you believe, and this is all I ask. People of Israel saw God and still did not always obey. You believe without seeing. Your belief will yield comfort, confidence, and obedience.

I love you, my child. You will feel my love, and you will feel love toward me. My love is healing. Pray for a greater flow of my love through you.

Build Our Relationship through Prayer—Let's Talk

† "Hear my voice when I call, O Lord; be merciful to me and answer me." (Ps 27:7)

Bring all your concerns to me. Open the channels for us to talk. Break down those walls of self-imposed restrictions, the limitations on what you bring to me. Break free from the burden of governing yourself. You are too selective during your prayer time. Pray with your heart, with your spirit, not with your brain. Your brain is of the world, your heart is of the Spirit. Prayer is food for the spirit. You cannot be a spiritual being without prayer.

You pray little but expect so much. Pray more and be anxious about less.

The weight you feel in your chest is the burden of your thoughts. You talk to others about the challenges you are facing, even though they are powerless to help. Bring your challenges to me. I can help.

Pray for what you want, not what you think you should be asking for. Be passionate about your prayer requests. Show some emotion. Dig deep, from the depth of your heart, and cry out to me. This is the emotion, the intensity, the sincerity I desire.

Learning is more effective when there is interaction. How does a teacher feel when a student doesn't ask questions? I want interaction. I want demanding students.

Feel the releasing, promising power of prayer. A half hour of prayer every morning would be wonderful. You speak to me for half an hour, and I speak with you for half an hour. Don't just give me airtime, give me substance.

Praying for my will to be done in a certain situation gives me the authority to act on your behalf. If you limit the ask, I limit the give. Praying, and placing your trust in me, opens the door for me to help you. When you do not ask me, you are signaling you do not want my help.

You have thoughts I address, sometimes immediately, sometimes later. True conversation, one on one, is possible. Change your expectations from receiving unsolicited teachings to having a meaningful conversation. My guidance can be powerful in real time. This has happened on occasion, and it has surprised you. It is possible! I can give you specific, personal direction.

I will give you comfort when there is nothing you can do about your situation, and I will give you guidance when there is. You may decide to accept my advice or not. If you make a decision that is not pleasing to me, I will not turn my back on you. Your decisions may not please me, but you please me.

Prayers reflect your desires at a given time, and because of free will, your mind changes. I need to be certain of your will. If I answered all prayers the first time I heard the request, how chaotic would the world be? When there is urgency, prayers are answered immediately; other times persistence is necessary. Some people only pray in crisis situations; why not pray to avoid those circumstances?

Prayer Advice — Jesus Inspired

† "And when you pray, do not keep babbling like pagans, for they think they will be heard because of their many words. Do not be like them, for your Father knows what you need before you ask him." (Matt 6:7–8)

When you pray, concentrate. Do not babble or ramble on. Pray with a purpose. You are talking to the God of the universe. Treat prayer with great reverence. Kneel, concentrate, be intense, passionate. You are in his presence. Do not be lazy, be respectful. Show God your commitment and sincerity.

You do not have to pray out loud. When you pray out loud, you have a tendency to be too deliberate. God wants your unfiltered thoughts; he likes to hear you think! People think much more eloquently and sincerely.

Prayer is difficult to conceptualize sometimes. Don't know what to say? Find yourself saying the same thing over and over? If you feel you have nothing to pray about, pray with praise and thanksgiving. Pray for others. Follow this advice to get started:

- Dedicate the time.
- Get into prayer-time position.
- Ask the Holy Spirit to help you pray.
- Keep a prayer book.
- Praise first, then give thanks, then ask.

The devil plants doubt during prayer. And why not? It's the most threatening time for him. He wants you to think your prayers are meaningless, that the Holy Spirit is silent.

Your prayer life reflects your belief in God. How much emphasis do you place on prayer? How much confidence do you have in the power of prayer? Do you give God an out such as, "If it is your will, Lord"? God doesn't need an out.

Either pray and believe you will receive or don't bother asking. Pray boldly and expect miraculous results. You work so hard for God without his help. Try asking for his help!

How many view prayer as a waste of time, telling God what he already knows, without the expectation of two-way communication? This does sound burdensome and meaningless! This misconception is constantly reinforced, even in churches, as they recite prayers out of routine and ritual.

Insight: "If we put so little heart into our prayers, we cannot expect God to put much heart into answering them."[5]

What Motivates Your Prayer Life?

† "You do not have, because you do not ask God. When you ask, you do not receive, because you ask with wrong motives, that you may spend what you get on your pleasures." (James 4:2d–3)

When you pray, what are your motives? Do you pray for tangible items, or do you pray for guidance, trusting I will provide what you need?

Be bold when asking for something that is righteous. I certainly would not withhold a dream from you, especially if it glorifies my kingdom. Do not think for one second I would withhold something righteous from you. I have desires for you too.

You pray for others, but you do not pray for yourself. You continue to internalize your own needs. Force yourself to think about what you want for your life, not to be selfish, but to give yourself some direction. Make a list of the true desires of your heart, not a fantasy list.

Do you feel unworthy to receive my gifts? Do you fear how you would react if you asked me for something and did not receive? Do you, therefore, limit your ask? Do you only ask for things that are safe, things you know I can handle?

Do you fear if your prayers are not answered, you may lose the confidence to pray? Do not let fear kill your motivation to pray. This fear is of Satan. Ask me to help you remove this obstacle.

Give Praise and Thanks

† "If you, then, though you are evil, know how to give good gifts to your children, how much more will your Father in heaven give good gifts to those who ask him!" (Matt 7:11)

Give praise and thanks in everything you do; this encourages further blessings. "Praise God from whom all blessings flow." This is not a song of praise but a song of instruction! Praise, praise, praise.

How do you feel when you give something away and do not receive a thank you? Aren't you more likely to keep giving, and giving more generously, if your gifts are appreciated, and you receive gratitude in return? So it is with my blessings.

Through the receipt of praise, I am more willing to give. Through the receipt of abundant praise, I am more willing to give generously. So should you, through the giving of praise, be more expectant to receive.

As a child, you received gifts from your grandparents when you visited. Did you receive those gifts out of works done or because of the love of your grandparents? Did you earn the right through your deeds to receive gifts from them? No, you were deemed worthy because of your love and your appreciation.

I give you this prayer of thanks. Use it and share it with others.

Prayer: "I thank you, Lord, for your Spirit that is within me, for the wisdom given me by the Holy Spirit, for my relationship with Jesus.

"Thank you for your constant presence. For being with me when I come to you, evidenced by your peace and comfort, and often by your words of guidance and wisdom.

"Thank you for allowing me, during this time of quiet, to completely forget about this world and its troubles, and focus only on you and your comfort. I thank you for revealing Jesus and for revealing the Holy Spirit.

"Thank you for the promise of forgiveness and salvation. I thank you for your love given and not earned, for my righteousness not deserved, and my salvation through no works of my own, other than believing in your son Jesus Christ."

Ask, and You Shall Receive

✝ "This is the confidence we have in approaching God: that if we ask anything according to his will, he hears us. And if we know that he hears us—whatever we ask—we know that we have what we asked of him." (1 John 5:14–15)

✝ "Ask and it will be given to you; seek and you will find; knock and the door will be opened to you. For everyone who asks receives; he who seeks finds; and to him who knocks, the door will be opened." (Matt 7:7–8)

✝ "Then the Father will give you whatever you ask in my name." (John 15:16b)

I am your loving Father. I have compassion. I hear your prayers, and I will answer them according to my will. When you ask for my will on a decision, I will guide you. I won't leave you stranded to figure out everything on your own.

Do not pray for the means to get there, for my ways are not your ways, and my thoughts are not your thoughts.

Come to me with your daily decisions. I can ease the burden of decision-making. Pray for safe travel home from work today. Pray for a good idea for dinner. What does it matter? No decision is too small or too large to ask me.

Believe So You May Receive

Believe that when you ask, you will receive. You can pray all you want, but if you don't believe, you won't receive. Prayers from your heart will be answered in my time!

Sometimes you pray for what you want, and I deliver something you never imagined. You'll look back and say, "I can't believe I prayed for that! Look how simpleminded I was!" You do not know what I am capable of doing.

Concentrate on receiving answers. How often do your expectations create reality? Low expectations create defeat, underachievement, disappointment. High expectations create success and excitement. Come to me with a high level of expectation and excitement.

Impact of Prayer

When you pray for changes to yourself—this is easy. These answers come from the fruits of our relationship. Ask for peace when your life is unnerving. Ask for guidance when you are lost. Ask for healing. Ask for strength and courage. Ask for patience.

Ask to better yourself through a deeper understanding of me, a deeper relationship with me. When you ask for wisdom and understanding, I give you wisdom and understanding. These requests will always be answered. I can change your life.

When you ask to change the world, it is more complicated. It takes time to move the world. Actions take time, for everyone and everything you pray about. One part of the world must be willing to change, and the rest of the world must be prepared to embrace that change. There are few simple fixes.

The actions of a single person have many consequences; they affect people unbeknownst to the decision maker. You do not know all the implications even a small decision may have; you cannot know. Only I can see the breadth of the impact, and I make good in all situations.

Prayer Builds Trust

As you ask, you will receive, and this will build trust. Regular prayer builds trust. Trust is earned. Let me earn it if I must.

You are a child asking for my favor. How long do you wait to grant your children's requests? If they are stuck in a hole, you act instantly to free them. If they ask for a new toy, you may wait to see if they ask again, to measure their desire.

If you were to receive without asking, wouldn't you view my gifts as coincidence? If your child asks for five dollars at the amusement park to buy an ice-cream cone and you give the money as a gift, then your child recognizes the gift and the giver, and it builds the relationship. If instead, you place a five-dollar bill on the ground for your child to find, it is luck. In both situations, your child received your gift, but only one example helped strengthen a relationship. In fact, finding the money diminishes the relationship because your child did not need to ask; it was just circumstance, and no bond was formed.

RELATIONSHIP— PERSONAL REFLECTION

† "Then God said, 'Let *us* make man in *our* image, in *our* likeness, and let them rule over…all the creatures that move along the ground.'" (Gen 1:26)

Created in God's Image

When I first read the Bible, I completely missed the impact of this verse. It has since become one of my biggest epiphanies.

First, the verse does not say, "I made man in my own image," it says let *us* make man in *our* own image. To me, this would imply at least one other being existed, whether this is referencing the preincarnate Jesus or the Holy Spirit, or both. I'll leave this theological debate for others.

The second part of the verse, "in our own likeness," is more important to me. We could interpret this as a physical similarity, but this is highly unlikely. I'm sure we have a number of similar characteristics to God, but one of special relevance to this book is emotional similarity.

God shares the same emotions we feel every day. We can analyze our earthly emotions and relationships to better understand how God feels toward us.

He is our Father, as we are parents to our children. How we feel about our children, on a good day, is how he feels about us every day. Are our children excited to see us and be with us? How does this make us feel?

How do we feel when someone ignores us? That's how God feels when we ignore him. How do we feel when someone we love apologizes to us for doing something which hurt us? That's how God feels when we confess to him. How do we feel when someone tells us they love us? That's how God feels when we love him. God appreciates praise the same as we appreciate praise. We were made in his likeness.

Nanny and Poppop

When it came to their grandchildren, my father's parents were exceptional givers, particularly my grandmother. We called her Nanny. She was the spoiler.

Christmas at Nanny and Poppop's house was pandemonium. The annual scene involving seven grandchildren tearing through millions of presents at the same time must have been chaos for my parents and my aunt and uncle, but my grandparents loved it. Every year.

When we stayed for evening dinner, Nan would turn our plates upside down to hide a special treat she placed on the table for each of the grandchildren.

God revealed a lesson regarding Nan's giving. Did we do anything to deserve a million presents at Christmas? No. Did we do anything to earn the special dinner treat? No. But we were excited, and we were appreciative, and we all loved Nan, and this is what mattered most. We did nothing to earn her love; she gave because she loved us unconditionally.

God gives us gifts all the time. I'm convinced the more praise we offer, the more blessings we receive. He enjoys our delight in those gifts, and he rejoices when we praise his giving and love him…like we do when we give! Praise God and accept his blessings with joy.

Insight: "Remember there are no limits to My giving—there may be to your accepting."[6]

Fear and Respect

† "Endure hardship as discipline; God is treating you as sons. For what son is not disciplined by his father? If you are not disciplined (and everyone undergoes discipline), then you are illegitimate children and not true sons. Moreover, we have all had human fathers who disciplined us and we respected them for it. How much more should we submit to the Father of our spirits and live! Our fathers disciplined us for a little while as they thought best; but God disciplines us for our good, that we may share in his holiness." (Heb 12:7–10)

I feared making my father angry when I was a child. He never used force to discipline me, but he knew how to keep me in line. I also loved him unconditionally, and of course, I still do. I feared him and loved him at the same time. We also need to fear God and love him. It sounds like a contradiction until you compare it to a similar human relationship.

The definition of fear transitions as we grow closer to God. Fear changes from a fear of harm and condemnation to filial fear, defined as humble, reverent respect and the desire to please, as one should have for one's own parents or grandparents, perhaps.

Do not let the new definition supersede or replace the old. God is still God. He refuses to tolerate sin and is capable of condemnation. However, the definition of fear evolves, so condemnation becomes less worrisome, and the awe and respect overshadow all else.

Our relationships with our parents, spouses, and children evolve over time. So does our relationship with God. It should never stagnate, never stay the same. If it does, we're not spending enough time developing the relationship. A couple's conversation during their first date is much different than after twenty years of marriage.

The evolution takes place because we gain wisdom with time and experience. As we become parents, we recognize what our parents sacrificed. As we learn more about God, we have a greater appreciation for the depth of his love. Without the relational maturity, we cannot make the emotional transition.

Your relationship with God will continue to mature, and you will feel this intimacy. It won't happen overnight. Your continued communication and obedience will strengthen your relationship, and he will become your best personal companion. The fear you once felt will turn to respect. Your inhibitions will lessen; your relationship will grow exponentially.

We have barely begun our journey together. This is the tip of the iceberg. The tip of the iceberg is the only section of the entire iceberg that is visible. The bulk of the iceberg is yet unseen, and its entirety is unknown from the surface.

It Takes Two

Insight: "God is interested in your prayers because he is interested in you. Whatever matters to you is a priority for his attention. Nothing in the universe matters as much to him as what is going on in your life this day."[7]

It takes two people to have a relationship, and both parties need to contribute to keeping the connection strong. God spends a lot of time in this chapter talking about prayer, and I'm not sure much needs to be added. Pray diligently. Pray with expectation. Pray big and pray small. Nothing is unimportant to God if it is important to you.

Pray the Lord breaks down your prayer inhibitions, that he gives you the courage to come freely, trustingly, completely. How would your prayer life be different if Jesus were sitting next to you, praying with you? Isn't he with you? Why do we make it any more complicated?

Ask God to fully explain and demonstrate the power of prayer. Pray for the guidance and the fellowship of the Holy Spirit. Pray for oneness with the Spirit who is available to you through God's grace and mercy. Pray for the Holy Spirit to embrace you and make you whole, one with the Heavenly Father—a clear channel of communication and love, knowledge and wisdom, direction and discernment. When you receive this, your days will be peaceful, joyous, and glorifying to God.

The benefits of prayer go far beyond communication, asking and receiving. Practicing daily prayer leads to a healthier life! Scientific studies confirm prayer reduces stress and aggression and improves self-control. There are physiological benefits, which include calming and healing.

Prayer creates a closeness with God, a sense of unity and trust that fine-tunes our spirit's sensitivity to the divine. Prayer also makes us more empathetic to the world around us; when we pray for people, we tune our spirit to their joys and sorrows.

Power of Prayer

I sound confident in my endorsement for maintaining an active prayer life. But this was not always the truth. I was confident in my communication with God, and my relationship with God grew very strong, but there was one big exception: I wasn't a big believer in the power of prayer. I'd say routine prayers. I'd pray for small stuff. The Holy Spirit prayed effectively on my behalf, but I never challenged God to prove the power of prayer for anything important. Never.

I wanted to witness on God's behalf, but how could I confidently lead prayer without the experiential evidence prayer works? My brain needed proof! I clearly realized the availability of communication, but communicating is much different than asking and believing I will receive. I had written plenty about the power of prayer, but I had not personally experienced it...yet.

From my journal:

* * *

I am going through a tough time. I am bombarded with life. I do not enjoy my job. I miss Florida weather. All my hobbies are outdoor activities, but the Rochester weather confines me indoors. I enjoy riding motorcycles, bicycling, boating, fishing, swimming in the ocean, getting a tan. I've lived in

Rochester for nineteen years, and now it seems like a sentence, not a life.

I'm aging. My financial picture is not improving. I realize this business won't lead to the financial windfall I hoped fourteen years ago when I founded the company. I should be planning for retirement. My friends are retiring. I'm raising two little girls and barely paying the bills, let alone saving for my golden years. I don't have the money to get my book published.

I'm not good at hiding my unhappiness. My wife wants me to get professional help for depression. I don't think it's depression; it's life. The clock is running, and I'm losing. I'm dragging my family into my abyss, and I can't fix it, and there are no timeouts.

It's time to give God the prayer challenge. There is nothing I can do about my situation. I've been patient, trusting God would help me without specifically asking. I haven't panicked, but my circumstances have worsened.

You have the opportunity to influence the direction of your future through prayer, or you can leave your future to circumstance.

You need to learn the power of prayer. There is not a single story in your book evidencing the power of prayer. You cannot go into this world on my behalf without this confidence about prayer.

All the information you need to know concerning prayer is in the Bible. You are searching for more, a deeper awareness. You understand the concept completely. You don't need any more research. You need practice.

Your book is developing into a wonderful work while your life is a mess. You talk to everyone about your job frustrations except me, the one with the ability to do something about it!

A man's job is vital to a man. You never prayed for the success of your business. Now you are missing the satisfaction of your work. You have never been this apathetic towards your job!

You have no motivation. The only upside to you for a well-performing company is self-preservation. You have never been in this position. You have always been driven to please someone, but there is no one to please. Minimizing your dissatisfaction is not motivating.

You have a list for everything. Make a running prayer list. Some items will be short-term, some long-term. Hold me accountable for my list. This is how you can organize your life again; make me part of it. You will witness the power of prayer, and this will make you complete.

So, I made a to-do list for God. I pulled out the stops. I gave him the full test, the final exam. And for the first time in my life, I was confident he would complete.

I reviewed the list with God every day. I pleaded, "Please let me know when action is required on my part, Lord. Otherwise, I will trust you are working on the list and clearing the path."

One week later, God addressed the list:

You are right in the middle of a very busy stretch of life. Stay calm, pace yourself. Think of me to calm you during the day. One day at a time. I am working on my list for you.

Do not begin to add more to your day than you already have. The world is swirling around you like a hurricane. Stay in the eye. The winds will come and go. Remain steadfast and know I am guiding you.

Five weeks later, my company elected not to renew my employment agreement for the upcoming year. I had ninety-one days to decide whether to accept their proposed new contract or find another job. Fourteen years of building this company hung in the balance.

I was going to trust God. This was all on his list.

Was this God's way of forcing me to make a change? I couldn't remember the last time I interviewed for a job!

I immediately contacted my network of industry professionals. I planted many seeds, remembering God's advice to cooperate and not coordinate. If this was God's plan, I was going to give him my best effort.

I initially received interest, but nothing serious.

Seventy-five days left to decide, and I had this conversation with God during the week:

"Thank you, Lord, for taking control of my life, for taking my prayer list and making things happen, even though I am totally scared as changes are occurring.

I may not have a job. I don't know what direction you are heading. But I could not have imagined the sequence of events over the past two weeks. I was blindsided by the non-extension of my contract, but I am confident you are in control."

Nothing is more important than prayer. It is our lifeblood.

Prayer is not just about asking and receiving. You can only ask for things you know to ask for. What about things you do not know? Prayer builds a bond to protect you against the unforeseen as well. Pray for my protection against the unforeseen. There are many more things which are unknown than are known.

You are like a child who is focused on immediate needs. Children do not know a fraction of the sacrifices a parent makes on their behalf to care for them, prepare the future, protect them. They cannot know.

When you place all your trust in the one who can do all things, your burden is light. I will give you what you need when you need it.

The following week, I felt compelled to open *Listen, the Lord*. I asked God where to start. He said, "Why not today's date?" The book is organized by daily readings. I turned to page 134, October 19.

Insight: Be willing to meet the demands of those who call upon you more often in quiet prayer at home and say to them, "My faith is so great in His power in prayer that I will do a better thing for you. I will pray." [8]

Not only did I have little confidence my prayers would be answered, I also never asked anyone if I could pray for them. Wouldn't it be wonderful to ask someone if they needed me to pray for them, and actually believe I could help!

God began to reveal the power of prayer in miraculous ways. I regretted wasting years on routine prayers without the real expectation of them being fulfilled.

Two weeks later, and only fifty-three days until the end of my employment, I received disappointing news on a possible job opportunity, and I expressed my concern to God:

"Heavenly Father, I cannot describe my disappointment today. My faith took a tremendous blow. I am completely discouraged and confused by your ways. Please, Lord, show me your will in this time of complete darkness. Show me the light, some light, so I know I am on the right path. Right now, I feel alone. Lost in the dark. The bad is far outpacing the good, and I trusted it would be the other way around."

Coming to me daily will save your life. You have no control over your circumstances. You are troubled by events that will take place in the future. If you trust me, then show it.

I learned of an upcoming industry conference in Arizona. I had previously decided not to attend because I had just returned from a weeklong meeting in Washington, DC. Now, with this new turn of events, I felt the urge to register. I found presentations that looked interesting, and I could socialize with my industry friends.

I called the program host to put me on a waiting list for a hotel room at the conference center. He paid my attendance fee, and I made my airline reservation.

The day before the opening of the convention, the host notified me of a vacancy at the convention hotel. This was ideal. Staying at an off-site hotel would have been distracting and would have reduced the meeting's effectiveness, and my time to network.

I woke early the first morning on East Coast time, several hours before the opening of the conference. I decided to spend time with God, and we had the following brief exchange:

"Please help me to learn how to trust you. If there has ever been a time in my life for this lesson, it is now."

What do you fear?

"I fear making the wrong decisions. Not being able to pay my bills. Weighing the option of further committing to a job I don't enjoy or choosing unemployment and hoping for an opportunity to arise."

You are going to get your answer this morning. Follow my will day by day, and allow me to work the plan. I know what you want to do. Let me put it into place.

With renewed enthusiasm, I fired off emails and texts to former colleagues as feelers for employment. I felt the time pressure build, and I became braver with my requests and more open about my situation. Plus, if God said I was going to get my answer, then I better send as many emails as possible!

When I exhausted my contacts, I headed to the meeting. This was a relatively new conference for me, with fresh topics and presenters. I learned a lot during the morning sessions. The diversity was good.

I met my small circle of friends but did not recognize most of the attendees.

Around midday, I caught a short break in the agenda and headed to my room to rest until the next presentation. This luxury would not have been available if I were not staying at the hotel.

I walked through the lobby and heard my name. The familiar voice was a former coworker from my Florida days, who was now president of a large national chain of wholesale auto auctions.

After a quick reunion, I downloaded my career dilemma. He asked for particulars and said he could help. We exchanged emails, and I was hopeful.

When the conference was over, I returned to Rochester.

With the clock ticking, my company pressured me to make a decision, assuming I was powerless to pursue an alternative at this late date.

But thanks to my impromptu visit to Arizona, the last-minute hotel vacancy, and my random lobby meeting with an old friend, I started my new job in Orlando, Florida, on January 1, the day after my old contract expired. I wasn't powerless. I was empowered by the one who took over my to-do list! God completed every item on his list, and I learned the power of prayer.

And since you are reading this, I obviously found a way to get the book published.

Fatal Flaw

Insight: "What's troubling to some Christians today is that Jesus's example of what prayer should be—a conversation with God—has become an example of what prayer should not be: mindless repetition. Many Christians today recite the Lord's Prayer in every worship service. It's a ritual. And it's so familiar that some Christians try to fly this prayer to heaven on automatic pilot."[9]

Church serves a magnificent purpose. I love church. Weekly attendance is vital for learning, worship, involvement in fellowship groups, prayer groups, outreach programs, youth programs, and community service.

We must surround ourselves with people who bring us closer to God. I love fellowship with other Christians, singing and rejoicing and praising God. My spirit gets recharged, and it feels great. It builds core strength.

We must continue to volunteer and support the church and our communities with all our energy and resources. We need to spread the Word and make people aware of God's love.

But I must ask this question: *do you have a relationship with God, or do you have a relationship with the church?* Confusing them is a fatal mistake.

The church cannot answer your prayers. The church cannot forgive you. Routinely going to church every Sunday will not punch your ticket to eternal life. Performing weekly church rituals is not building a relationship with God. Speaking with the head of your church is not confessing to God. Even though the church is the bride of Jesus, it is not a substitute for Christ.

Do not confuse the acts of humans with the sacred holiness of the Trinity. The Catholic Church teaches there is one intercessor between God and man—Jesus Christ. Mary was the mother of Jesus, but she cannot forgive your sins. The saints were wonderful Christians whose faith and courage we should aspire to emulate, but they were also human. Do not extend your veneration of Jesus' mother or the saints beyond what the Bible authorizes. This is the first commandment: worship the one and only true God.

Science is not Christianity. Idols are not Christianity. Worshipping prophets and preachers is not Christianity.

I could attack all religions and rituals by referencing biblical support or lack thereof, but I'm not writing to make enemies. I'm making the distinction between Bible-based Christianity and other religions to make a point, and this should be perfectly clear: Your salvation is possible *because, and only because,* of Jesus Christ's sacrifice on the cross, his resurrection, and your belief and confession that he is your Lord and Savior. Do not confuse having a relationship with the church with having a relationship with God.

Satan would love the degradation of Christianity because of failing or misleading churches. He would love for us to idly attend church and go through the robotic, repetitive rituals, developing a superficial and fragile relationship with God. He loves our confusion between having religion and having a relationship.

Don't follow rituals not supported by the Bible and think they make you righteous. When in doubt, put your trust in God. Develop an intimate relationship with him, in quiet, during the week, every day, one on one, and allow him to reveal the truth so you may be secure in your faith.

* * *

Church is important. It's a time for fellowship with other Christians. It's an opportunity for me to strengthen your faith. Don't go to church for the flesh but for the spirit. Your spirit needs to be recharged, as well.

Be the spiritual leader of your household. Your family needs the discipline of church and will embrace the fellowship. Surround yourself with Christians who can help you in your journey. Live for this time, not without it.

STEP 6

LOVE

† "Therefore, love is the fulfillment of the law." (Rom 13:10b)

† "I love those who love me, and those who seek me find me." (Prov 8:17)

† "How great is the love the Father has lavished on us, that we should be called children of God! And that is what we are!" (1 John 3:1a, b)

Unconditional Love Defined

Love comes from an intimate relationship, which few develop because few seek. My love within you is to be shared with others. Sharing is love and the one true measure of a person's goodness. Love supersedes all else.

Love comes from the heart and needs no convincing. It is innate, it defies logic, it cannot be explained. It is a feeling, not a thought. Love cannot be forced; it must be felt. Love is developed, not taught.

The need to earn love on earth is required sometimes, but this is not unconditional love. This is contingent love. Love is contingent upon doing deeds. The more deeds you do, the more love you receive. You can never have too much love. Therefore, you can never do enough deeds. This is a terrible burden to bear.

Learn of my unconditional love. I can show you heavenly love, everlasting love. A perpetual love that does not get too busy, does not get angry with you, does not criticize you, gives you peace, relieves your burden, gives you patience, and lifts the yoke of the world off your shoulders.

I know love because I am love. Accept my love, rely on my love. Love me with all your heart, and love each other. My will is for you to love me, and you will be able to say, "I love Jesus."

Love is beautiful, love defeats anger, love defeats Satan, Satan hates love.

Do not let worldly distractions interfere with your ability to love. Love is a priority. Love brings great joy.

Do not forsake the love of others. Do not cast the love of others aside or take it for granted. It is rare and precious. However, it is still human love; a love which is fragile, fleeting, unpredictable, conditional.

See the difference between human love and my love? Human love is wonderful, but it is temporary. Human love touches the surface. My love embraces your core. Do not vie for human attention but for divine attention.

Feel the Joy!

I want you to enjoy life, but you must exercise enjoyment with godly discipline, not earthly abandonment. My love will bring you joy. Love life to the fullest, live today to the fullest, live in Christ, and receive his joy.

Life on earth is tough, and joy does not abound. Sometimes you must look for joy. Joy can come from the appreciation of the simplest things, such as the beautiful morning singing of the common robin. Such extraordinary sounds! Find joy when and where you can!

True joy can only enter a guiltless heart. Forgive yourself for whatever gives you guilt. Ask for my forgiveness, then give it to yourself.

Love Thy Neighbor

† "Dear friends, let us love one another, for love comes from God. Everyone who loves has been born of God and knows God."
(1 John 4:7)

Love the stranger, not only the ones who love you.

Love your neighbor. This is your neighbor at work, your neighbor in the checkout line, your neighbor in the car beside you on the highway, your neighbor regardless of what you are doing. Your neighbor is every man, woman, and child. Bring your neighbors to me through your actions.

Be a blessing to those around you. Be open and free in your communication with others, so they may see me in you. You can be a witness for my love. It may flow through you to others. Slow down and spend more time loving and caring for others. Love others as you want to be loved.

Often it is more important to listen than it is to speak. Speak louder with your actions. Express your love freely through your actions. Showing love is love, not telling love.

You cannot always choose the people you meet or the situations you face, though you can choose to love each person and make the best of each situation. I may have placed them in your care! You may be the answer to their prayer!

Do not judge. Judging, criticizing, and mocking is not love. Do not mock the less fortunate, for you may be likewise humbled.

Forgiveness Defined

Forgiveness is the act of loving someone despite the occurrence of an unloving act on their part. Forgiveness transcends all other human emotions and actions. Forgiving love is the true test of the strength of the heart. Forgiveness takes love to a whole new level.

I forgive because I love unconditionally. You cannot comprehend my grace and mercy. I know you will make mistakes. But because I love you and know you are human, I know they are just mistakes.

Forgive and Forget

Many times, the source of a leaky roof is an unloving act performed by someone you love. The act can be many forms; words, actions, reactions. The pain is amplified because of your relationship and may create a long-lasting, unfavorable psychological affect.

You must forgive those who have caused you pain. Tell me you forgive them so I may heal your heart. Cleanse your heart by demonstrating a forgiving heart. Lift the forgiveness up to me so you can rest and have peace.

Telling someone you forgive them when they know they have wronged you is extremely powerful. It may not seem so at the time you tell them, but it will touch their heart and make a difference, as long as you truly forgive them with your heart.

Bring to me those who have wronged you unknowingly and allow me to open their eyes. Pray for them and pray for yourself, so you may be cleansed by your forgiveness and your trust in me to heal you.

Do not go to bed angry at someone you love. Do not let the anger fester. Anger is of Satan. Do what you can to reconcile and allow me to do the rest. I will give you peace and release your anger. Do not lie dormant, doing nothing, with anger in your heart.

Unforgiveness is a terrible burden. Forgiving is cleansing. Forgiveness will set you free. Too many people forgive but do not completely release the hurtful memories, so they must continue to forgive and forgive and forgive. Forgive and forget. Move on.

Your Precious Heart

† "You will seek me and find me when you seek me with all your heart." (Jer 29:13)

I know your heart is good. It is precious to me. Your heart was lost, and now it is found. Your heart is mine, and mine is yours.

Protect your heart. You cannot love me with all your heart if part of your heart is hardened from unconfessed sin, consumed by anger, jealousy, regret. Ask for forgiveness and healing of these conditions, so your heart might be restored to purity.

Purification of the heart does not require a conscious action on your part. It comes naturally from me, as a result of our ongoing fellowship. You may think, "I did nothing today to purify my heart." But you did. You dedicated yourself to me and wrote these words, an act which further cleansed your heart.

LOVE — PERSONAL REFLECTION

God is Love

† "Whoever does not love does not know God, because God is love." (1 John 4:8)

† "But God demonstrates his own love for us in this: While we were still sinners, Christ died for us." (Rom 5:8)

It is not possible for us to comprehend the extent of God's love. God's love is described as everlasting, unfailing. We can talk of unconditional love and pretend we understand, but we can only relate with our earthly minds and hearts. Can we conceive of having unconditional love for every human being?

Picture the most despicable, sinful human being; a murderer of children, a terrorist who detonates himself in a crowd, a violent rapist, the most ungodly, unrighteous person. Imagine then voluntarily, brutally sacrificing your own child to save this person's life.

I'll be honest: that won't be me.

But this is the sacrifice God made for us, and his forgiveness is available to those who recognize and accept this sacrifice.

God is Forgiveness

† "For if you forgive men when they sin against you, your heavenly Father will also forgive you. But if you do not forgive men their sins, your Father will not forgive your sins." (Matt 6:14–15)

God taught us the importance of forgiving others. Forgiveness is a tremendous act of love. The preceding passage was from the Sermon on the Mount. The first verse (Matt 6:14) validates our reward for forgiving others: we receive God's forgiveness.

Matthew 6:15 concerns me. If *we do not* forgive others, *God will not* forgive our sins. The Bible is clear that our belief and only our belief in Christ Jesus is required for salvation, and Jesus's death on the cross and resurrection paid for our sins. Other than accepting this truth, I did not think any other human act was required for salvation. Is this a contradiction?

Another scary thing about the second verse is that God puts us in his shoes. God, the ultimate source of forgiveness, empowers and requires his followers to forgive as he forgives. Thus the statement applies to God as much as to us. Can you imagine God not forgiving someone? No way!

When we accept Jesus Christ as our personal Lord and Savior and are filled with God's Spirit, it should be natural to forgive others as God forgives. We must allow God's Spirit to carry out his work in us, so we may represent God to the world.

Are we capable of not sinning? Are we capable of completely forgiving everyone? The answer to both is clearly no. As Christians, however, we would like not to sin, and we would like to forgive, but as humans, we are not capable.

However, *refusing* to forgive is the same as refusing to stop sinning. This is not consistent with the behavior of one who has received salvation, or for anyone the Holy Spirit dwells within.

It is our *desire* not to sin and our *desire* to forgive, which allows us to pursue a closer relationship with God. Likewise, our *refusal* to stop sinning and our *refusal* to forgive will distance us from God and subject us to the wrath of Matthew 6:15.

In either case, we need God's help. In the Lord's Prayer, Matthew 6:12, the petition is for forgiveness of debts as we forgive the debts of others. Receiving forgiveness is conditional; it requires us to forgive others.

In conclusion, of the eleven stages in developing a relationship with God, love comes early, at number six. Knowing forgiveness is a deeper state of love, it would appear more difficult to further our intimacy with God with unforgiveness in our heart. In other words, the move up the spiritual staircase, past step six, will be harder, or impossible, to climb.

Unforgiveness in our heart can be cleansed by God, but it requires us to take the initiative. We must ask God to cleanse our heart of unforgiveness so we may continue to grow spiritually. Again, would God deny the answer to this prayer, knowing we are seeking further intimacy? No!

Loving Jesus — Part 1 — My Struggle to Love Jesus

I reflected earlier on my childhood church attendance, and the mimicking antics my father and I would employ to keep me entertained. Here's a silly example: I would scratch my nose, and he would scratch his nose. I would cross my legs, and he would cross his legs. He'd jab me, I'd jab him back.

This would continue until one of two events; either Mom would give us both a dirty look, or we'd be giggling so loud we threatened to disrupt the service. This was a fun childhood memory with my dad that, until recently, I completely forgot.

Fast-forward from my childhood to my time on the lake and the point to this story. I always had a tough time saying, "I love Jesus." Honestly, I did not feel like I knew Jesus, so how could I love him? Maybe it was a man thing.

Mom told me to view Jesus as a brother, that kind of love. I could not trick my mind into creating a brotherly love when it did not feel genuine. After my salvation, when I began to communicate and receive messages from God, the concept of loving Jesus was still a big obstacle.

How was I possibly going to overcome this inhibition? I tried to learn everything I could about Jesus. I read books and watched movies about his life on earth. I read the Gospels over and over. I found they helped me to know Jesus's life better, but they did not improve my intimacy with Jesus. I clearly knew of his love for others, but I did not feel it for myself.

Why do we place the burden on ourselves to accomplish tasks which should be left for God? I worked so hard at trying to feel love for Jesus! This was a formidable stumbling block for me to overcome, and it prevented my spiritual growth. It never occurred to me that God also desired this intimacy and could easily remove this obstacle, which he finally did.

Loving Jesus — Part 2 — My Jesus Vision

One day at the lake, I prepared for quiet time. I opened the curtains on the bedroom window to view the shimmering ripples on the water in the morning sunlight and placed all my materials on the bed. It was customary for me to lie on the bed on my side, with my elbow on the bed and my arm bent upward, supporting my head.

This morning, I was at the top of my bed, lying across the bed, with my back resting against the pillows, facing the foot of the bed with my eyes closed.

I paused to pray and settle into the comfort of my devotion time.

Instantly, I opened my eyes and saw an image of Jesus, lying at the foot of the bed, with his head resting in his hand, looking right at me, exactly mimicking my position. He smiled and disappeared—that quickly.

I remember the goose bumps, the tears in my eyes.

I responded, "There you are!"

I closed and opened my eyes again to see if he would reappear, but he didn't.

I know Jesus wasn't in my room in physical form; the bed didn't move. It was a vision, but I felt like he was actually there for a second or two.

I couldn't have scripted a more perfect introduction. He was intentionally mimicking me, a playfulness I hadn't remembered for forty-five years since my church days with Dad. Jesus reached back to recreate a memory from my childhood I would instantly recognize, with a little sense of humor. In that moment, I knew he had always been with me.

The encounter was abundantly comforting. An inexplicable sense of peace radiated through my body. The vision conjured so much emotion in a split second. I knew Jesus was in complete control. Everything was real and true and okay. There was a calming confidence in his smile; it was engaging and reassuring.

I can always look back on the occasion and smile. I can't wait to see him again, to tell him I love him. This experience changed my life and my relationship with Jesus forever. Now I can picture Jesus and be with him whenever I want. A simple vision brought so much reassurance and completely erased any possible lingering doubt about Jesus' existence.

Just as no two people are the same, no two experiences with Jesus are the same. Do not hear my account and expect the exact same thing to happen to you. How personal would that be? This vision was specifically delivered for me, as your experiences will be unique for you.

Loving Jesus — Part 3 — No Shortcuts Are Available

Prior to my vision of Jesus, I was frustrated with my inability to love Jesus. Everyone at church seemed to love Jesus. Alleluia. Amen! I didn't share their enthusiasm. I tried but couldn't.

Then I noticed something while editing this book, which I need to insert here. Back in the chapter on awareness, which was a conversation between God and me about ten years ago, God said to me, "You must know Jesus before you can love him. Your love for Jesus is not something you develop, but something he develops within you arising from your obedience and the maturation of your relationship."

This was perfect. Because of my obedience, God chose a vision to connect me with Jesus. As God promised, my relationship matured through ongoing communication and fellowship, and Jesus revealed himself.

If we desire an intimate relationship with God, but we have been disobedient, or we have sinned, or maybe we have unforgiveness in our hearts, God will reveal those weaknesses, eliminate those obstacles, and open the door for us to grow closer to him. This will take time, and we must be patient.

We cannot unilaterally force ourselves to love Jesus. I tried, and it didn't work. Now that I know the steps of spiritual maturity, I understand why. I tried to move love (step six) up around salvation somewhere, skipping over communication (step four) and relationship (step five). I was trying to love Jesus before I knew him.

Once again, I don't want to categorically generalize about how someone should feel. Everyone's experiences will be different. I don't know how to explain love. But I'm fortunate to know what love feels like in a human sense, and I wanted the same sensation with Jesus!

Only through the evolution of our relationship was God able to impart his intimacy and deliver his perfect vision. As much as I wanted to shorten the process, like in a human relationship, I could not love someone I did not know.

How Loving Are We?

God is love; therefore, we should also be love. Loving others is one of God's fundamental guidelines. We will surely be held accountable for the measure of our love on judgment day.

What motivates our actions on earth? Is our kindness really performed out of love for others, or is it self-preservation, or even self-promotion? Are we genuine or superficial in our efforts to demonstrate God's love? Do we love others only when others were watching? Do we volunteer our time or donate money out of obligation or because of love? When you ask yourself these questions, how does the Holy Spirit within you respond? What do you feel in your heart? Do you feel the Holy Spirit confirming your good intentions, or do you feel guilty? When judgment day comes, are you confident you will receive God's approval? Since God and the Holy Spirit are one, you may have just received your answer!

STEP 7

TRUST

† "Those who know your name will trust in you, for you, Lord, have never forsaken those who seek you." (Ps 9:10)

† "May he give you the desire of your heart and make all your plans succeed." (Ps 20:4)

This story of Joshua teaches us a lot about trust:

"And the Lord said to Joshua, 'Today I will begin to exalt you in the eyes of all Israel, so they may know that I am with you as I was with Moses. Tell the priests who carry the ark of the covenant: 'When you reach the edge of the Jordan's waters, go and stand in the river.'"

"So, when the people broke camp to cross the Jordan, the priests carrying the ark of the covenant went ahead of them. Now the Jordan is at flood stage all during harvest. Yet as soon as the priests who carried the ark reached the Jordan and their feet touched the water's edge, the water from upstream stopped flowing. It piled up in a heap a great distance away....The priests who carried the ark of the covenant of the Lord stood firm on dry ground in the middle of the Jordan, while all Israel passed by until the whole nation had completed the crossing on dry ground." (Josh 3:7–8, 14–17)

Unconditional Trust—Jesus Inspired

Can you give God your unconditional trust? You believe with your whole heart, but do you trust with your whole heart? Trusting no matter the circumstances or possible outcomes?

There are different levels of trust. Conditional trust—I trust you as long as… or unconditional trust—I trust you no matter what! Unconditional trust allows you to put your foot into the Jordan River, while suspending the sacred ark of the covenant, and expect the water to stop flowing.

God is trustworthy, yet few place their unconditional trust in him. It is through increased faith that you will give him your whole heart. Pray for increased faith.

Why don't you entirely trust God to lead you in everything you do? Fear that he will ask too much of you? He may lead you down a path you don't want to go? Your interests at this time may not be perfectly aligned? Maybe the busyness of life precludes you from asking? Do you claim to know what is better for you than God? Not sure if God can handle the task?

Liken yourself to an infant who screams and resists medicines and vaccines. Are you not an infant compared to God? Can you possibly know what is best for you?

Complete trust comes with complete spiritual maturity—the full development of the relationship. There are no shortcuts when it comes to completely trusting God.

Unconditional Trust—God Inspired

† "To you, O Lord, I lift up my soul; in you I trust, O my God. Do not let me be put to shame, nor let my enemies triumph over me." (Ps 25:1–2)

You are vulnerable because you have opened yourself up to me. There is much good and much evil surrounding you. Ask for my guidance and heed my advice. There will always be opportunities for you to stumble, but I will not allow it. Step out in faith despite the fear. Trust my hand will keep you from harm.

You believe in me. But do you trust me? When you learn to trust me completely, there will be no fear. Fear fills the void which complete trust should fill. Doubt causes fear.

Have no doubt about my faithfulness to you. I love you, my child, and I will teach you to trust me completely...a concept foreign to your nature.

Pray more and think less. The first thing you should do is to give me your concerns, not the last thing. If you can't completely trust me, the perfect provider, how will you ever trust anyone?

People go through periods of transition in their lives. Do they turn to me or from me when these changes occur? Most people, when they face difficulty, come to me. You do the opposite. It pains me to see you try to figure out everything on your own when I know I can help you.

Your lack of unconditional trust is not because you doubt me. You do not release control over the situation. Sometimes you hold even tighter during the toughest times as if to say, "This one is too difficult for God, too much to consider. I better take this one myself!"

You trust me when failure is inconsequential. That way, if it doesn't work out the way you want, you say, "Hey, it wasn't too important anyway!"

You trust me in an emergency or as a last resort. "I'm powerless, and/or I've tried everything—one or the other. And since I can't do it, here you go, Lord, please handle this one."

Source of Mistrust Revealed

Trusting someone does not make them trustworthy. Trusting humans unconditionally will lead to heartbreak when this trust is broken.

My trust is true; I will never forsake you. I will never ever break your trust. Peace will come to you with complete trust and obedience to me.

You are not trusting because you do not see yourself as trustworthy. You are the person you viewed as the most trustworthy person in the world, but you let yourself down when you broke your wife's trust. Until you restore trust in yourself, you will not regain your ability to trust. When you trust someone completely, mistrust never enters your mind.

Ask forgiveness from those you have wronged. You must admit and confess you broke their trust. The identification of that act, the recognition by them that you have acknowledged your wrong, restores their faith in you.

Trust Me, I Can Do It Better!

† "Trust in the Lord with all your heart and lean not on your own understanding; in all your ways acknowledge him, and he will make your paths straight." (Prov 3:5–6)

Nobody on earth has all the answers. Everyone has issues and concerns. Yours are easy; they are self-inflicted. Your self-will has brought you here. There are so many worse problems in the world people are enduring. Put yours into the proper perspective. This is not condemning; this is the truth.

You only trust yourself. "In order to do something right, I have to do it myself." Trust me, I can do it better. Trust me one day at a time. Comfort yourself that we will make the right decisions at the right time. Do not try to figure out my ways. Ignore your perception of wrong or right, good or bad. They are feelings of the flesh, perceptions with little faith and limited understanding.

You look at your circumstances and say, "I don't know how you are going to do this, Lord." But I know. You cannot know. It is far beyond you.

I do not cause the stresses of life on earth. Let me be the one your world revolves around, and your stresses will lessen. I will not disappoint you. I am steady love, steady support, never changing. I am the rock.

Do you trust, or do you hope? Hoping is wishing. Trusting is believing. Hoping is not a strong sign of faith. "I hope and pray" is not a powerful statement of trust.

Expectation is proof of trust. When you trust someone, you expect them to behave a certain way. If you trust your children, you will expect them to do the right thing. Trust me, and I will exceed your expectations.

You Worry Too Much

† "Who of you by worrying can add a single hour to his life?" (Matt 6:27)

† "Therefore do not worry about tomorrow, for tomorrow will worry about itself. Each day has enough trouble of its own." (Matt 6:34)

† "Then Jesus said to his disciples: 'Therefore I tell you, do not worry about your life, what you will eat; or about your body, what you will wear.'" (Luke 12:22)

† "Come to me, all you who are weary and burdened, and I will give you rest." (Matt 11:28)

Do not worry about the future. Do not worry about tomorrow, next week, next month. For when the time comes, your worries may prove pointless, meaningless, a waste of time, a needless distraction.

Jesus did not even know where he would lay his head each night. Isn't it most important to have today what you need today? Do you really know what you will need tomorrow? Circumstances change daily. Trust me, you will have what you need. If you hoard money, are there any guarantees you will not lose it? If you give it away, how do you know you will not get it back tomorrow tenfold? What you don't have can always be given to you, and what you do have can be taken away.

You continue to worry, and this worry burdens you mentally and physically. A worried mind cannot be fruitful. How can I reduce my stress at work? How can I earn more money? How can I pay for my kid's college? Where am I going to live? How am I going to get through this winter?

What do you worry about that you think I can't control? You are uncomfortable because you do not know where your life is headed. You have always had a master plan; now, you don't. I have a plan, but you are not mentally ready to let yourself be dependent on my plan.

You view your life as complicated and worrisome; others view the same life as blessed. As one life may be both, which do you choose to emphasize? Do you look to the future with excitement? If not, how do you change your outlook? Why do people continue their current paths of monotony? What can you do today, so you can be excited about tomorrow?

Now is not the time to decide what to do for the rest of your life. You waste too much time trying to figure out your own answers. When I, knowing your will, knowing the future, can accomplish so much more, so perfectly, if you trust me and allow me.

Give me your day today! Replace worry with prayer. Prayer is the only way to place your worries and fears onto my list of responsibilities, so you may concentrate on fulfilling my purpose. Fulfill the tasks that further my kingdom, and I will make sure your earthly obligations are met.

Faith Away Your Worries

Short-term issues create time pressure, which creates worry. That's life. Maintain the inner faith that although short-term concerns and challenges will come and go, you will prevail for the greater good through me, your Lord and Savior.

Worry is fear. Fear not, for I am with you. Worry and fear are major distractions. They consume valuable time, of which you have so little. If you sense fear, stop and rest; be with me until you regain your strength and then go fight again. Worry and fear signal mistrust.

Your faith is like the lake, deep in some areas and shallow in other areas. On the surface, your commitment to me often changes, influenced by the wind in varying intensities and direction.

Be more like a river, constantly running downstream with great force, forging on despite the presence of rocks and other obstacles. Rivers continue to flow in the same direction as if they have a purpose.

Continue to build your core strength through faith. Core strength grows weak from the worries of the day. Core strength is the necessary foundation for long-term growth. How you handle short-term, daily challenges either consumes your core strength or adds to it.

You ask for good grades for your son at college. You are willing to make sure all he needs to worry about is grades. As long as he performs, you will handle the finances and other obligations, which otherwise would distract from his ability to be successful. Do you think he worries if you will fulfill your commitment to him?

The key is to believe I will satisfy my commitment to you. Trust me to open doors and close doors for you. Have the faith to go past the doors that are closed and through the doors which are open.

Past, Present, Future

Do not regret the past, do not worry about today, do not fear the future. Your mind is full of regrets. Regrets are from Satan. They are history. Mistakes are building blocks. Cast away regrets in my name. Regret, worry, fear, unforgiveness are all of Satan. Do not let these emotions interfere with our relationship. Do not let these burdens ruin your life.

Say, "I will not regret, I will not worry, I will not fear, for the Lord is with me."

TRUST — PERSONAL REFLECTION

Tough questions about trust:

- How do we grow to trust God to lead us every day?
- How do we eliminate fear and worry, so we can feel God's protection and love?
- How do we learn patience and accept that events happen in God's time?
- When will we realize if we ask, we will receive?
- How many coincidences are necessary before we realize they aren't so coincidental?
- How does this transition happen, so we will completely trust that God has everything under control?

Me, Myself, and I

You've heard the expression, "I only trust three people: me, myself, and I."

Building trust takes time. I've never trusted anyone on the first handshake. Some people immediately trust folks they meet. For others, it takes more time. These differences stem from prior experiences of either successful relationships or heartbreaks.

I felt I was the most trustworthy person in the world until my marriage fell apart. Now I don't trust myself. I'm sure most of us have let someone down in our lives, someone who trusted us. The biggest guilt for me comes from breaking trust, probably because trust requires investing so much time and personal effort to earn.

There are degrees of trust. "I'll trust you to pick out a nice restaurant for dinner tonight" requires far less nerve than trusting someone to pack your parachute. If we don't entirely trust someone with the task, we double-check what they did, or we simply do it ourselves.

I've been fortunate in my life to be greatly loved by my parents; the rarest form of unconditional love reserved for children. I trust my parents unconditionally. There's one problem; they're not omniscient. I'd trust them to pick out a good restaurant or even pack my parachute, but would they be the best choice to help with long-term career decisions? How about marriage advice or how to identify and fix addictions or personal conflicts?

My parents offer great advice, but they cannot possibly know the outcome of all decisions; they can only advise based on their knowledge of earthly circumstances. On the other hand, God knows the future. He knows the outcomes from making the right or wrong decisions and the impact they may have on others. There is no guessing with God.

Trusting God is important, but don't get lazy and assume God is taking care of everything for us. Like the woman praying incessantly to find a husband, yet she stays at home and watches television, never leaving the house to meet anyone. Part of the solution requires action on our part; we must leave the comfort of our house and allow ourselves to be guided. Help God help us.

> Do not pray in substitute for action on your part. Pray in conjunction with action. Don't refuse the rescue boat I send to you because you are praying for the floodwater to stop rising. Your effort is required, no doubt about it.

God talks about unconditional trust; the confidence to trust God no matter the degree of difficulty. Jesus says in John 14:1, "Do not let your hearts be troubled. Trust in God; trust also in me."

How do we attain the faith of Daniel, the trust in God to save us from the lions? As with human trust, it is developed over time with the maturation of the relationship. Unconditional trust involves no backup plans, no second-guessing, no doubt, just trust God has everything under control.

Insight: "Remember always, doubts delay. Are you trusting all to Me or not?"[10]

Insight: "All your doubts arrest My work. You must not doubt. I died to save you from sin and doubt and worry. You must believe in Me absolutely."[11]

God builds the trust. He will prove he can be trusted in your life. He will create the apparent coincidences to solve your problems, answer your questions, or allow you to make the right personal connections. It may not happen when you expect it to, and it may not be what you had in mind, but it will be perfect.

I Would Have Answered Ten

Insight: "Put all fear of the future aside. Know that you will be led. Know that you will be shown. I have promised.[12] When fears assail you, and cares trouble you, then it is because you have ventured out of that protecting Shadow."[13]

I was on the treadmill at the gym watching a game show, and the question was asked, "On a scale of one to ten, how much time do you spend worrying about the future?" The top answer was ten, the most amount of time, among the hundred people surveyed.

It's tragic we bear the burden of self-dependency. We spend too much time worrying about the future. We make plans, backup plans, and then contingency plans. We try to figure out everything on our own!

I find myself praying for little things, trying to figure out the tough decisions on my own. The bigger the job, the more I tackle myself! This is ridiculous! Why would I possibly think I can do *anything* better than God?

I'm not trying to minimize our difficulties or oversimplify the solution. The burdens we bear as humans in this imperfect world are real and can seem insurmountable. I don't see my issues as small or short-term. As the CEO of a large company, a husband, and a father of four, many of the decisions I make have a long-lasting impact on my life and others.

The following prayers from my journal occurred over several months. You can see my struggle with worry as I repeatedly prayed to understand the concept of trusting God.

* * *

"Lord, is it possible trust is the key to giving you my whole heart? I don't understand the concept of giving you my whole heart, and you ask for it constantly. If you want my whole heart, you must teach me how to give it to you."

* * *

"Father God, please show me a sign I am following your will, so I may feel reassurance and be comfortable releasing these thoughts and worries from my mind. Please teach me to trust you completely, without reservations or conditions. I am sure I have never completely trusted anyone or anything. I always have a backup plan."

* * *

"I've put myself in a position where I have little choice anymore but to trust you will take care of me. In your perfect timing, Lord, your will be done. I will not pretend to know more than you, the God of the entire universe, what is best for me. I pray for solutions to specific issues of personal concern and ask for your expeditious resolution, as these items weigh heavy on my heart.

"I also want perfect timing, so if the answer is not forthcoming shortly, please give me patience.

"I want your blessing on my relationships, my job, and my future, so give and take as you please. Harden hearts and soften hearts, open doors and close doors. I will obey. I trust you know my desires and will consider them. I trust you know what is best for me and what is not.

"I trust you see the future and have a perfect plan. Please make your will obvious and give me the courage to obey."

Don't Feel Stranded

During my struggle to completely trust God, I woke up one weekday morning, determined I was going to have a worry-free day. I was going to trust God to take care of me. I was going to enjoy the day and have a positive attitude. "I'm not going to worry today. Let's see what happens!"

Here's how that day went.

I decided to drive my motorcycle to work and have a little fun. It was a beautiful day for a ride, a rare Rochester sunny day, with no rain in sight. I had a nine o'clock conference call, so I woke up early and packed my gear.

Unfortunately, my briefcase, laptop, and gym bag did not fit into the bike's storage. I got frustrated, trying to jam everything into the saddle-bags in all different directions. I was determined to make this work because I had dressed for the ride. I did not want to change clothes, take off my boots, put on a suit, and get in a car.

I finally strapped the gym bag to the sissy bar with bungee cords and was on my way to work. Of course, during all this maneuvering, all geared up, I began sweating, which only exacerbated my impatience. But I was now moving and looking forward to a nice ride.

I had two close encounters at the first two intersections. Cars shot into the street without stopping; right-hand turns, no looking, no yielding or seeing me. Okay, no harm, no foul. Without further incident, I turned north onto the main highway heading through town, when the bike began to sputter and finally stalled. The cycle had run out of gas! At least I wasn't in a remote spot! I passed a gas station about a quarter-mile back, so I figured I could push the bike.

Stupid idea.

Plan B—I decided to walk to the gas station. Surely they would have a gas can I could borrow. I would get enough gas into the bike to drive back to the station, return the can, top off the tank, and continue my ride to work.

This plan worked fine until I could not get the fuel from the borrowed one-gallon can into the motorcycle's tank. There was a spout on the can, but it did not work properly. Gas spilled onto the hot engine and onto my jeans and boots.

Fortunately, enough fuel went into the tank to get the motorcycle started. Steady traffic prevented an easy U-turn, especially with a gas can now in my lap. I started to pull into traffic and realized I forgot to put on my helmet and goggles. I'm sure you're starting to get the picture… Plan B was not going too smoothly.

I arrived at the gas station and inserted my credit card. The credit card did not work, so I hustled forward to the next pump. This pump didn't work either. The message on the pump read, "see cashier," so I pushed the bike back to the previous pump, the first one I tried.

By now, the clerk was sensing my frustration, so he must have activated the pump from inside the station. (Mind you, this was the same clerk who loaned me that fine gas can.)

I thanked the attendant when he stuck his head out the front door and yelled for me to "lift the handle and pump."

Ah, gas was flowing.

He yelled out the front door again, "Your credit card didn't work! You need to come in and pay cash."

Of course!

Normally, I would not have considered this a good start to the day. But I honestly found some humor in the situation and kept a good attitude, remembering my morning resolve to give my day to God. When I presented my cash, the clerk said, "Not having a very good day, huh?"

I replied with hope, "Not yet."

I arrived at work with five minutes to spare before my call.

The obstacles were many, but I was persistent in my faith, and my lesson on trust was timely. This turned out to be a silly, harmless experience, but I was nonetheless pleased I stayed calm and even laughed at the adversity.

Trusting God does not mean you will not have obstacles, but in the long run, God's timing is perfect, and he will not leave you stranded.

No Such Thing as Coincidence

Experience tells me coincidences are generally good. I'm more of the belief events happen for a reason, so, to me, coincidences aren't so coincidental. Sometimes God chooses to validate decisions or learnings with other supporting material or experiences. We may view them as coincidences. I prefer to view coincidences as confirmations, particularly when they glorify God!

The following three stories are all unique and occur over a five-year period during my journey, evidence that God interjects his signature periodically as continuous reinforcement of his presence. If we are receptive to recognizing his handiwork, these apparent coincidences can validate his guidance and reinforce our trust.

* * *

Thursday, April 9, 2009. I entered Easter weekend alone for the first time with my newfound focus, and I was led to read Psalm 22. Granted, this is not an uncommon chapter for anyone to read, but to me, at the time, this psalm was no different than any other psalm.

I learned the following day, Good Friday, this psalm was David's premonition of the original, forthcoming Good Friday. God set the stage for the weekend. It was incredible to be innocently led to the chapter which so succinctly predicts the crucifixion story. Because God led me to these verses, the entire Easter weekend was a new experience for me. I internalized the swing of emotions during the weekend, beginning with the last supper on Thursday night, the subsequent betrayal, the pain of the crucifixion events, and the glory of the resurrection on Easter Sunday. I was purposely led to Psalm 22 with perfect timing.

* * *

I was glued to Christian talk radio during 2011, especially interested in the aptly named Bible wars. I greatly admire folks who have devoted their lives to learning and interpreting every verse in the Bible. Radio listeners called with questions, and the show host spontaneously answered by reciting Bible verses verbatim.

I was so intimidated; I questioned my own spiritual maturity. Even though I desired to write a book and speak publicly on the Lord's behalf, I decided not to continue without receiving a sure sign from God. I wanted to share what I learned and help others facing the same challenges I was experiencing. But after hearing these profound Bible scholars, I felt completely inadequate, and I second-guessed my motives. How could I be impactful with so little knowledge of the Bible?

One of the more interesting speakers and well-versed Bible educators on the Family Radio network was pastor Harold Camping. He became well known for his predictions of the end-times, first during September of 1994 and again on May 21, 2011, which was quickly approaching.

I listened intently (every day for several months) as listeners would call the radio station and challenge Mr. Camping. He was very skilled at Bible bantering, and the debates were engaging.

Was it appropriate to predict a date? I am certain the Bible says we will not know the day of Jesus's coming.

One day during this time frame, I had a frustrating morning. My journal entry that day reads as follows:

Inspiration is absent. Even the Bible readings are a chore. This is one of those mornings when nothing seems to click. I prayed, read the Bible, and read my daily devotionals. I woke up early this Saturday morning for quiet time, now it seems more like a waste of time.

I have so much on my mind. I know it is my fault. There are a lot of distractions. Even my pens don't work! Two pens died writing one paragraph! I began this morning in a spiritual drought, again.

* * *

Then I reread the last ten days of notes and realized how wrong I was, how powerful God's messages had been! How quickly I doubted myself! Satan can place doubt and negativity in our minds so quickly!

God also led me to the following passages:

† "No one knows about that day or hour, not even the angels in heaven, nor the Son, but only the Father." (Matt 24:36)

† "Therefore keep watch, because you do not know on what day your Lord will come." (Matt 24:42)

† "So you also must be ready, because the Son of Man will come at an hour when you do not expect him." (Matt 24:44)

† "But the day of the Lord will come like a thief." (2 Pet 3:10a)

Then on my way to work, the Family Life Radio station, not the same as Camping's Family Radio, spoke about Matthew 24:36, 24:42, and 24:44! These were the same passages I studied and wrote in my book minutes earlier. They referenced Ecclesiastes 8:5, "And the wise heart will know the proper time and procedure." I also looked at Ecclesiastes 8:17 and read, "Even if a wise man claims he knows it, he cannot really comprehend it."

This radio discussion was not in response to Mr. Camping's teachings but was perfectly relevant for me. Through this alternate forum, God revealed his answer regarding the end-times.

God also reassured me I was hearing perfectly by providing the corresponding Bible verses. It was the proof I needed to minimize my insecurity with respect to technical Bible knowledge.

These coincidences convinced me, once again, to pursue my dream to write a book to glorify God.

And, of course, the world did not end, again.

* * *

I was in the market for a late-model, American-made motorcycle—a cruiser; one of the big ones, with the bags, radio, cruise control, all the accessories. About three months ago, I bid $17,000 at a wholesale auto auction, but my high bid was not enough for the seller. After learning the seller's reserve price, I passed on buying the motorcycle.

Recently, a similar motorcycle became available online. The asking price was $20,500, and the bike had low miles. The owner lived about seven miles from my house.

After a few emails with the seller, I made an appointment to see the bike. When I arrived at the seller's house, a lady named Lois greeted me. I was, of course, surprised to be greeted on the front lawn by a friendly woman, instead of a big, burly, tattooed biker guy. And I'm sure she was glad to see me, tattoo-less and not accompanied by a gang.

Lois greeted me by explaining the bike was her late husband's. He had passed away suddenly from a brain aneurysm. This stopped me in my tracks, and I offered my condolences. It was truly surreal, as I mentally transitioned from the anxiety of possibly negotiating with a hard-core biker dude to consoling a recent widow confronted with selling her husband's prized possession.

I asked Lois about her best price, to which she replied, "I really can't take less than $17,000!" The adjusted price was a good deal for this bike, so we shook hands.

She was thrilled when I said I'd buy it, and I was equally as thrilled to buy the bike for the exact price I had mentally committed to pay several months ago for the motorcycle at the auction. Sometimes you have to recognize God's handiwork and say, "Yes."

Lois said how blessed she felt, knowing the bike was going to a good home, and her husband would approve. Then, for some reason, she told me she was a Christian.

I replied, "I am a Christian too."

She shared that her husband was charismatic.

I asked, "So he spoke in another tongue?"

"Yes," she answered.

We had a lot in common. I explained my mother is charismatic; she uses a prayer language also.

Lois asked where I attended church. I responded that I recently began attending Northridge Church in Webster. She said this was her church also! She hadn't attended recently, admitting she felt mad at God.

Neither of us could comprehend why bad events happen to good people. I offered that God has a purpose in all things, and if you ignore him, you will never know what his purpose might be. For instance, he is the one who put us together!

I don't think I ever ministered to anyone with more confidence in my life. It was a natural flow of God's words to Lois. We hugged and cried, and the motorcycle became peripheral.

I told her I was writing a book about having a relationship with God, and she was going to be in it! I told her where I sit at church and said I hoped she'd join me! We agreed there was no such thing as a coincidence.

STEP 8

OBEDIENCE

† "Trust in the Lord with all your heart and lean not on your own understanding; in all your ways acknowledge him, and he will make your paths straight." (Prov 3:5–6)

† "A man's steps are directed by the Lord. How then can anyone understand his own way?" (Prov 20:24)

Obedience 101

Your obedience is evidence of your love for me. I know the goodness in your heart. Your heart is not pure, but your desire to purify your heart is sincere.

In the past, you would never have said, "Your will be done." You feared losing what you felt was important. There were things you were not willing to forego. But I see a sincerity now which did not exist before.

Doing my will is sacrificial. It may not feel like it to you right now because you enjoy what you are doing. But you are making sacrifices, nonetheless. I do not like to see my people suffer, so I will lead you in a way that is manageable. You will want to follow me. You will know it's the right thing to do, without question.

I will care for you and protect you with every step. There will be no surprises. You will not hear me say, "Oops, I didn't think of that." You will make mistakes, but your continued faithfulness will overcome them.

Desire My Will

Desire to do my will with all your heart. The effort is much easier when the heart is resolved. Be excited with anticipation, because my desires for your life are wonderful.

When you ask for my will to be done, you must be willing to obey. Ask me daily how you can help, then miracles will happen. This is how our wills become aligned. Your will becomes my will, my will becomes your will. Following my will daily leads to a lifetime of obedience.

Follow my urges. Obey my subtle commands. Keep your mind, mouth, and actions holy. Glorify me by discouraging what is evil. It will be easier with time and a strong resolve, which you will receive from me.

Obey My Will

Our daily time together is fruitful. It shows your desire to listen. But your obedience is challenged greatly when asked to perform. What good is guidance if you do not obey? It takes no courage to listen and write. It takes courage to trust me. Pray for the courage to obey.

You must listen, trust, and obey. You want to fulfill my purpose, but all you do with confidence right now is listen. Eventually, you trust, and eventually, you obey, but on your terms and not mine.

I am not asking you to be like a dog on a leash. This is not willing obedience. I will not put a figurative leash around your neck. That is the law, the Old Testament. If anything, I remove the leash and let you run. A dog freely released from his leash exhibits abounding joy. He runs and runs, simply to be free. Instinctively he returns, knowing the love and care that greet his obedience.

Know also the joy you feel as his master when your dog runs off, happy in his freedom. And the joy you feel when he returns, the satisfaction from his obedience and his desire to be with you.

Step by Step

When I say I will lead you step by step, I mean day by day. How can we plan for tomorrow when we must first see what you accomplish today?

Do not worry about yesterday or tomorrow. One cannot be changed, and one may not occur. Obey today's commands, so the path may be clear for tomorrow.

It is difficult for you to not look ahead, not plan, not be able to figure out life on your own. You give me options as if I need your suggestions! Backup plans are only necessary for worldly matters. The heavenly plan is the perfect plan and needs no backup.

Do not carry two days' burdens on the shoulders of one day. I realize your limits of tolerance. I will never ask for more than you can give.

I will cleanse your spirit step by step, and people will see a difference in you. I will open their eyes. You will not need to change them or open their eyes for them.

Changes in your behavior and attitude, no matter how slight or irrelevant you think they are, add up and make a difference. You may not recognize all the changes, but someday you will look back and realize the extent and wonderment of your journey.

My Will Is the Light

My will is perfect, it is my blessing. It involves my complete protection and guidance. The creator of the universe wants to help you and guide your life. Do you not think I will do a good job? Do you not think I can handle all your concerns? I created you. I can handle it.

My will is the path through the dense woods, and Jesus is the light. The Holy Spirit is your eyes and ears to help see the light and follow. He is part of you and is with you always.

If you could see through the woods, you would not need a guide. You cannot know which direction leads through the woods without being shown. You cannot see the clearing on your own, nor will you reach it on your own.

You might not see every step you take, what you might be stepping on or tripping over, but you will know the direction to go. You will navigate the big obstacles because the one carrying the light will help you over the fallen tree or through the narrow passage, holding the tree branches aside to protect you.

Beware of Detours

† "In the paths of the wicked lie thorns and snares, but he who guards his soul stays far from them." (Prov 22:5)

Display proper discernment. You will not be deceived to follow the wrong path if you are centered on me. Do not deviate from the path.

I do not lead my children down the wrong path. Do not mistake a new path for the wrong path. New paths lead to growth and new adventures. Uncomfortable and unfamiliar is not necessarily wrong or bad. I simply may have nudged you out of your routine.

Do not fear the unknown. Continue to walk the path with confidence and trust. If I am not walking with you, holding your hand, then I am ahead, clearing the way. You cannot follow the path without me leading you.

Satan is constantly blazing alternate paths for you to follow. Unlike my trails, Satan's paths have no trail markers. The path closes quickly, and you will not know which way to go. He also digs pits and sets snares baited with temptation on the path. Follow my light closely so the pits are visible and can be avoided.

When you become lost, Satan will not allow you to turn around and retrace the path you just traveled back to where you started. That matted trail is gone. This would be too easy! Since his path always leads away from mine, it is arduous to get back to my trail. Only through thick brush and thistles may you find your way back. Satan is good at making thistles and thorns. You must plow forward with determination to find my path again. When you do, I will help you heal. Pull the thistles from yourself, and prepare for the new path ahead. It is much easier than the detour you took.

You will have scars from your excursions, but scars no longer hurt; they are reminders of past wounds. Begin to walk down my path again, and you will lose sight of where you went astray. I am sorry about your pain, but they were not my thorns, not my will.

Obedience is Easier Than Disobedience

Disobedience causes stress. Spiritual warfare is an internal war you must win to become righteous and obedient. It wears down your mind and body. I know what you are battling, and I will not abandon you. When you are disobedient, I will forgive you. But you must move forward with stronger resolve.

To many, obey is another four-letter word to be avoided. People fear obedience. The burden of righteousness appears too overwhelming. I will ease your burden, so you can incorporate righteousness into your everyday life. It is a discipline, a choice. Achieve one challenge at a time. Resist one temptation at a time. Satisfaction from your obedience will encourage further righteousness. The more you trust in me and not your own understanding, the more comfortable you will be.

I reward obedience, which comes in two forms. Obedience through doing, and obedience through not doing, such as avoiding sin; breaking a pattern of sin in the name of obedience.

Your reward for these acts of obedience is fulfillment, feeling my love and presence. A fulfillment that is not earthly, but an internal feeling of peace and love so consuming that you feel the intimacy with Jesus.

Obeying is freeing. It breaks down walls. How much better is the feeling of freedom, through following my will, than the stress and bondage of doing what you know is not pleasing? You must experience one in order to fully appreciate the other. How often is this demonstrated in life?

Obeying is easier when you know the results will be pleasing. You must step out in faith and obey to learn this lesson. Eventually, you will seek so you can obey. Until then, it sounds frightening. If you continue to follow my lead, you will never say, "I wish I hadn't done that!"

Pruning

† "I am the true vine, and my Father is the gardener. He cuts off every branch in me that bears no fruit, while every branch that does bear fruit he prunes so that it will be even more fruitful." (John 15:1–2)

Obeying my will requires a lot of pruning. I will do the pruning. Pruning is cleansing. Pruning is essential for continued, healthy growth. You will look and feel ugly as the pruning is in process, but when I am done, you will be well groomed and ready to blossom like never before.

When a lot of pruning is necessary, sometimes big branches need to be cut out first. This eliminates the need to individually prune all the little stems and twigs on the big branch. After the big changes are made, the pruning shapes you for future growth.

It takes a while for a tree to recover from the removal of a big branch. If the branch was alive, there's usually a lot of sap. Be assured, the sap will wane, and the wound will heal.

Crying and fasting are emotionally, spiritually, and physically cleansing. There are times when the lessons learned require heartache and disappointment. Persevere through the suffering. It is part of the pruning process. Do not go back to what is wrong to reduce the pain. The hurt will eventually ease, and the wrong will be gone.

Fear Not

† "Peace I leave with you; my peace I give you. I do not give to you as the world gives. Do not let your hearts be troubled and do not be afraid." (John 14:27)

Want my will, with all your heart, unconditionally. You cannot have reservations about what I may ask of you. This doubt arrests me. Do not fear, for I already know your reservations and the real reasons for them.

You assume I will ask you to make tough decisions against your will. Don't be fearful about what I may require of you. I tell you the truth; your heart will rejoice when you experience my will being carried out in your life. Be open to receiving these blessings, not fearful. I want the best for you, my child.

Satan's most powerful instrument is fear. He wants you to fear, to be anxious about where I may be leading you. Fear will keep you from hearing and obeying me. As you look back, is there anything you have done, which I have asked you to do, that was fearful? Of course not. Trust me! There is no fear in you when you are in me.

I know of fear, but I do not fear. I also fear not for you because you are in my hands. Your fear stems from a lack of faith. You believe, but you do not entirely trust. I have led you through many difficult situations, mostly without you even knowing.

OBEDIENCE— PERSONAL REFLECTION

† "He replied, 'Blessed rather are those who hear the word of God and obey it.'" (Luke 11:28)

LET'S FACE IT, NO ONE likes to be told they must obey. Obedience sounds terribly sacrificial. The fear of meeting God's expectations is intimidating to a new Christian. After all, God's expectations are lofty! Committing yourself to become obedient is a very big step, but you will soon learn that it is completely fulfilling. I know this sounds like a contradiction, but as your relationship with God matures, your interests and priorities change because you want them to, and it is satisfying. One Saturday, I typed for eleven hours because I wanted to, not because God commanded me. When you are with God, and God is with you, obeying comes naturally.

The following three prayers are from my journal and reflect my transition from fearing obedience to enjoying obedience.

* * *

This first prayer occurred early in my journey when the *fear* of obedience was overwhelming:

"Please don't teach me obedience through harsh lessons. Please change my heart, Heavenly Father, so I may desire complete obedience, and feel joy, comfort, and peace with my decisions, and have no regrets. I am beginning to understand the end goal but still don't feel confident in my own ability to achieve complete obedience. I have the faith you will lead me, but I don't really see any improvements in my self-will."

* * *

The second prayer begged for discipline to be consistently obedient:

"Heavenly Father, please help me to make a total commitment to you. I find time to be in your presence, to read the Bible, to pray and be still, yet I feel empty and unfulfilled. I'm disobedient. My lifestyle does not reflect my faith. Please help me to overcome these inconsistencies so that I may progress in my development with you. I have the desire and not the willpower."

* * *

The third prayer was much later and clearly depicts a changed attitude toward obedience. I experienced God helping me become obedient, and realized this was an exercise we would perform together:

"I feel myself changing. I thought being a good Christian would be impossible; the effort would be overwhelming. Now I am beginning to sense an unconscious decision to behave in ways that further my knowledge and faith. I prefer to read the Bible, to listen to Christian radio. They give me comfort. It's more natural to me than the alternatives.

"I thank you, Lord, for you have blessed me with such great desire and wisdom. You have made me disciplined and obedient. In all you have guided me to do, never has there been a burden so great I can even remember. Your guidance is so gentle."

More Pruning

God's insight on pruning is also very powerful. The pruning of oneself is the transformation of your will to God's will, clearing your path toward obedience. Depending upon your starting point, you may be required to make some significant sacrifices to become obedient. Addictions, sexual tendencies or preferences, or other ungodly behaviors may need to change.

God will change you. He will mitigate the pain from the pruning of these undesirable traits. Yes, it may be painful for you or others, but you will welcome the change.

When my mother read the pruning parable, she added, "And the pruning will allow you to grow straighter and taller and closer to God."

Little Child on the Path

> † "Whether you turn to the right or to the left, your ears will hear a voice behind you, saying, 'This is the way; walk in it.'" (Isa 30:21)

I have an image of an elementary-age boy venturing innocently into an overgrown field of tall brush, surrounded in the distance by thick woods. He is cautious but unafraid to follow the narrow path of matted grasses which cut through the wilderness. He has no provisions as if he wandered onto the path by accident from the playground nearby.

Wearing a baseball cap, his hands in the pockets of his shorts, he curiously journeys down the path, too young to worry about what might be around the corner.

Because of his limited height, he can only see a short distance ahead. The growth on either side of the path appears full of thistles, surrounding the small child and seemingly reaching out to him. Beside the path, there are fallen logs, thorns, poison ivy, and worse. Yet he walks without concern, not knowing where the path leads, or what lies over the next knoll.

I liken this scene to our walk with God. We walk the path of obedience, trusting God will provide for us and clear a path that is manageable and safe.

But we are human, and we wander. Whatever the reason, we've all found ourselves off the path, lost and without direction. There is never an easy way back to the path. Inevitably there are consequences—scratches, some sort of bloodshed, rashes—and usually some level of regret. Clearly, the path of least resistance is God's path, laid out for us to follow, which we must innocently and obediently walk.

Thief Dream

† "Do not store up for yourselves treasures on earth, where moth and rust destroy, and where thieves break in and steal." (Matt 6:19)

When our personal "end of time" arrives, we should not be holding onto possessions while forsaking obedience to God.

Last night I had a dream I was robbed. The sliding door to the back patio was accidentally left open, and the thief took all my valuables. He stole items from my bedroom while I slept.

When I woke up, I was perplexed by the mystery of the theft, but I was not devastated by the loss of property. Possessions have always been important to me. They represent worthiness, a job well done, a reward for hard work. But I did not seem to mind that my valuables were gone.

I think the dream was a sign I had overcome my attachment to belongings, and I was beginning to peel myself away from my idols. This was a big accomplishment for me, considering my lifetime drive for success and the accumulation of worldly rewards.

I also sensed the thief was Satan. He was testing me to see how I would respond to being robbed and whether I really committed myself to Jesus.

Then, of course, there was this verse in Luke, which not so coincidentally was *the first thing I read the next morning during my quiet time with God!*

† "But understand this: If the owner of the house had known at what hour the thief was coming, he would not have let his house be broken into. You also must be ready, because the Son of Man will come at an hour when you do not expect him." (Luke 12:39–40)

Overcoming Self-Will

Our self-will is an immensely strong force to overcome. It fulfills the needs of the flesh and drives us to create earthly pleasure. When I originally moved to the lake, I was free to do whatever I wanted. My self-will was given the green light. But I was there for a reason: I wanted to learn God's will for my life. There was a fierce fight at times between my self-will and God's will.

Eventually, as I grew closer to God, our wills began to align, or rather my will began to look more like God's will. It was not "woe is me" sacrificial. I did not say, "I really want to do this today, but it is not God's will, so I won't."

God's will for our life is tailored to suit us, so we may enjoy life while we fulfill his will if we just become less stubborn and let him show us his plan!

Guided by the Holy Spirit—God Inspired

† "If you are guided by the Spirit, you won't obey your selfish desires." (Gal 5:16 CEV)

Recognize the difference between doing your will and doing my will. My will is revealed in our time in the mornings and through the Word. You will know when you are compromising my will. Difficulties arise when you knowingly follow your will contrary to my will. You will not have peace; you will have unrest. Perfect peace comes only through me and obeying my will.

When guided by the Holy Spirit, what you want to do will automatically be acceptable. What is not acceptable will become detestable. This is how you will know you are following my will.

* * *

I believe the Holy Spirit creates the passageway from self-will to God's will. I believe the Holy Spirit can cure the weakness of the flesh. Our desire to be obedient allows the Holy Spirit to begin his work in us, to help purify the flesh and guide us closer to God. The Holy Spirit is our inner voice that prompts us to do God's will and makes us feel guilty when we do not. His guidance becomes stronger with our continued obedience, and we soon find ourselves fulfilling God's purpose for our lives.

Insight: "Do you not know that each soul whose spirit seeks for Mine above all else, finds? There is no set rule, no ritual that is fixed, for any of My children who desire with all their hearts the gift of the Holy Spirit. But the hunger must come from the deep deepness within you."[14]

Uzzah the Example

Uzzah tried to prevent the ark of the covenant from tipping over, for which God took his life. Here is the story:

> "They moved the ark of God from Abinadab's house on a new cart, with Uzzah and Ahio guiding it. David and all the Israelites were celebrating with all their might before God, with songs and with harps, lyres, tambourines, cymbals, and trumpets.
>
> "When they came to the threshing floor of Kidon, Uzzah reached out his hand to steady the ark, because the oxen stumbled. The Lord's anger burned against Uzzah, and he struck him down because he had put his hand on the ark. So he died there before God." (1 Chr 13:7–10)

* * *

Uzzah steadied the ark of God with his hand when the oxen stumbled. God killed Uzzah for touching the ark. David became angry with God.

This perplexed me, so I decided to question God. Here is the brief conversation:

"Why, God? The Bible is your book. Why do some actions appear unreasonable? Uzzah was serving you, carrying the ark, working hard for the Lord. Why do you not fully explain actions like killing a seemingly obedient Uzzah? This does not appear to be just, and certainly not loving."

It was always understood that touching the ark of God was forbidden. I enforced my command. Notice in the next verse, "David feared God that day." Picture the scene, and the impact his punishment had on the witnesses.

David became a great leader, author of the most beautiful psalms through many firsthand encounters with my power and my love. How could the Psalms have been so eloquently written, expressive, and devoted if not through these experiences?

"And the lesson is? There must be a reason I have focused on this section all morning."

The lesson is obedience under any circumstance.

* * *

It was understood the ark of the covenant was the seat of God in the midst of the Israelites. It was divine, sacred, holy. Only appropriately sanctified people could touch the ark; anyone else who came in contact with the ark would die. This was common knowledge.

Uzzah did what any of us would have done; he reached out to prevent the ark from falling. But the minute he touched the ark, he signed his own death warrant. He was disobedient to the known rule of sacredness.

In our modern worldview, we do not adequately understand the ancient Hebrew concept of holiness. Uzzah's death had nothing to do with whether he did something wrong in a practical sense, but he did something wrong in the ritual and sacred sense.

Uzzah was immediately disciplined for his reaction to save the ark. How often do our disobedient actions result from reactions? This is a big part of "obedience under any circumstance." When we consciously choose to obey God and try not to sin, we are still subject to events that may require spontaneous restraint. This is a test of our level of maturity in the obedience realm. We must have the discipline to make the right choices when we don't have time to think about what is right or wrong. We need to instinctively be obedient.

I am abundantly thankful God is most interested in our desire to be obedient, otherwise I, for one, would be in big trouble.

Kneeling Vision

I was lying on my bed during quiet time with the bedroom curtains open. The early morning sun was rising above the eastern hills and reflected off the lake, shining brightly through the window. I closed my eyes and began to feel God's peace.

Suddenly, momentarily, I was looking down at my bedroom from above, through God's eyes. In this vision, I saw myself kneeling beside my bed with my back towards the window. My elbows rested on top of the covers. I was leaning slightly forward with my hands clenched and head bowed in earnest prayer. The shadows from the window mullions crisscrossed on the back of my shirt. I was praying obediently, oblivious to my surroundings. I was completely surrendered in a position of devotion, dedicating my time, my life, to God.

I don't think the vision was given to me for the visual aspect. I believe the purpose was for me to experience God's appreciation for my humbleness. I was seeing myself through God's eyes, and I felt his compassion. It was both visual and emotional. Because of this vision, I not only learned the importance of committing fully and obeying God, I felt it.

When you dedicate time to be in my presence, and you are truly interested in communion with me, then act like you are in the presence of God.

Practice What You Preach

Despite all I write about the best practices for a faithful and obedient Christian, I fell back into the trap of busyness. My daily time with God became monthly or worse.

The following experience occurred during a prolonged period of silence. Most of my notes had been penned by this point, but the book was far from finished. My free time was consumed by personal obligations, family events, and travel for work, and I struggled to prioritize God. I wanted to find time for God, and I felt him tugging at me, but I gave precedence to my other activities.

* * *

I was scheduled to travel to the East Coast for the entire week. Even though it was a business trip, I decided to resuscitate my faith during my downtime. I was determined to dedicate time every day to be with the Lord. I kept my promise, and God was clearly ready for my return! We had a wonderful reunion, which solidified my resolve to return to obedience.

Most significantly, one morning, I wrote the following inspirational message from God:

Practice what you preach. You do not lead the life you profess. You are my witness, so act like one. You wrote the book, you wear it (Christian T-shirts), you display it (Phil 4:13 wristband), now live it! You must initiate the path to progress. You must take the steps, open the door, begin to walk. I cannot lead you anywhere if you are not moving.

He was right. I was not leading the life I was writing about. A minute later, I picked up *Listen, the Lord* and opened to a random page, and was met with:

Insight: "Practice what you know. Work where you are then take the next step."[15]

It was a classic God move. He spoke the truth, then immediately confirmed his message from a different source. After all the time I was away from God, he came right back where we left off and hit me over the head with a spiritual club.

Okay, okay, practice what you preach, practice what you know. I get it. I had been stagnant in my communication with God, and I had not done a single thing to advance the book or practice my faith in months. God wasted no time calling me out!

The following morning was checkout day. I woke up at 6:15 a.m., well before my alarm. I dressed and went to the hotel gym, exercised and rode the stationary bicycle for an hour or more. I was at the gym alone, so I took my time and enjoyed a peaceful workout.

I returned to the room, took a shower, packed my suitcase, got dressed, and spread my books on the bed for quiet time. I got on my knees beside the bed, which I hadn't done in a long time, and I prayed for purity. I prayed aloud God would release my sin and remove my distractions. I prayed I would find the time to be with God regularly. And I prayed for the motivation to finish the book and for God to help me to practice what I preach.

"I want to practice what I preach, Lord."

The instant I spoke the words, "I want to practice what I preach," the bell-tower alarm from my phone sounded, startling me from my prayer zone. I turned off the alarm and collapsed on the bed in complete awe at the timing of it all. Three times in two days, God emphasized to "practice what I preach," under no uncertain terms!

Consider how much free time I had that morning—waking up early, getting ready for work, going to the gym, packing for another leg of travel, finally settling down for prayer! I never looked at the clock or was concerned about the time. I never thought about the alarm I set the night before.

God made his point in the most convincing manner. I was completely floored, completely in disbelief at the perfect timing of all these events and the certainty of God's message. God's handiwork was on full display. There was no question he precisely executed these coincidences. No question about it.

Sometimes you don't leave God's path; you stop on it. You are on his path but are just standing still. Over time, the brush and thistles from the surrounding area begin to grow into the path, reaching you and obscuring the path. You must keep moving. Do not let the path become overgrown due to your silence and indecision.

STEP 9

WISDOM

✝ "For the Lord gives wisdom, and from his mouth come knowledge and understanding." (Prov 2:6)

✝ "For wisdom will enter your heart, and knowledge will be pleasant to your soul." (Prov 2:10)

✝ "If any of you lacks wisdom, he should ask God, who gives generously to all without finding fault, and it will be given to him." (James 1:5)

Accepting Wisdom

A student attends college to learn a trade, as you are learning from me. You are gaining confidence in my wisdom, and you believe. You have the gift of understanding and believing. People struggle with believing.

My wisdom is perfect. It is available. Wisdom through our direct communication, wisdom from the Bible, wisdom from Jesus and the Holy Spirit. Your potential for learning is limitless; it has no boundaries because I have no boundaries.

My wisdom will become more personal over time. Not due to the element of time, but due to the growth of trust and intimacy, when sharing becomes easier and deeper—as in any relationship.

Study and learn what is currently in the world, the teaching and prophesying. Familiarize yourself with the Christian ministry environment, so you will better identify what is being taught, how it is taught, and equally important, what is not taught.

You will begin to see circumstances and people for what they are, with an unbiased view. I bring recognition to the subconscious acts of people.

I will lead you to people who can help you. Be aware of the opportunity when it knocks. Your growth will be greatly accelerated through these connections. You have nothing to be ashamed of or intimidated about; you are not spiritually inferior.

I want you to share this wisdom. Document the learnings from our time together so others will recognize the possibilities for themselves. My wisdom for them will be far different than my wisdom for you. You are writing to give guidance to others, and at the same time, you are learning about yourself. So it can be for everyone. Make sure this message is clear.

Bible Wisdom

People read many books during their lifetime, but how many have read the Bible? I mean really read it? Secular literature becomes popular then fades away, but my Word is everlasting, ever present.

Pray for understanding before reading the Bible. You will never be denied the answer to this prayer. Ask the Holy Spirit to bless your readings. He knows the Bible! He will give you insight as you open the pages.

You may question whether you hear me correctly, but do not question the written Word. Do you believe the Bible? Without the Bible, your faith is without foundation.

Your reading does not have to be structured and orderly. Enjoy the Psalms of David. They will appear new every time because of your deeper consciousness. Read the Gospels and feel the love of Jesus. Read and rejoice in my Word, however you feel compelled!

Do not force your way through the Bible to get to the end. When you eliminate the burden of duty, the Bible becomes a whole different experience. You won't be reading for the sake of reading but for understanding.

I may speak to you through the Bible to make sure my message is clear. The Bible will answer your questions. It is exciting when scripture stands out and grabs your attention. It is not a mistake. These are special occasions led by the Holy Spirit. Embrace these moments and rest assured, these are divine and unique for you.

Bible wars are common; different interpretations and teachings from the Bible. Do not become part of the debate. Discern your own truth based on your learnings and what you feel in your heart.

What you witness should be supported by scripture to build credibility for you and credibility for your message. Never pretend to be someone you are not, or to know something you do not. Do not add words to my words. Speak about what you know, not about what you don't know.

WISDOM—PERSONAL REFLECTION

† "'For my thoughts are not your thoughts, neither are your ways my ways,' declares the Lord." (Isa 55:8)

SEEK GOD'S WISDOM FOR YOUR personal spiritual development and discernment. Pray for wisdom to overcome obstacles preventing you from growing closer to God. Sometimes the simplest and most obvious insight can only be revealed by God.

God's wisdom can be delivered in many ways. Gain spiritual wisdom from scripture. Learn the gifts of the Holy Spirit—speaking in tongues, visions, dreams, interpretations of tongues, and prophecy. Rereading old notes may create new inspiration. Days, weeks, or months might pass, and I'd receive an entirely new interpretation. Sometimes I found a corroborating message or Bible verse which explained everything, such as this experience from my journal:

After two weeks of writing thoughts that were seemingly incoherent, unimportant, and disconnected, I am confused. I experienced two weeks of doubt, two weeks of wondering whether I was hearing from God or not. Nothing makes sense. My faith is being tested.

It can only be described as divine that today I found a book at a secondhand store in an airport, addressing everything I have written over the last two weeks. My exact thoughts and scripture passages were discussed and reinforced in a little paperback published three decades ago.

The doubt and confusion quickly became a distant memory.

Q & A with God

I could never have identified my own insecurities and tendencies without God's help. After he exposed my psychological issues, my guilt was extinguished, so I included them in this book despite the embarrassing personal content. God gave me the courage to take this risk. I'm at the point of my spiritual maturity where it is more important to share this intimate exchange than protect my pride.

Here are some specific examples of God's infinite wisdom and his willingness to reveal truths, of which I would otherwise be unaware. Fortunately, because of the following revelations, I no longer fear the motives behind these feelings.

I asked several personal questions and immediately received…nothing! Weeks passed until finally, out of nowhere, God revealed the following responses. This exchange is from my journal that day:

"Father God, I have questions about my personality that bother me and force me to question my core values, morals, and habits. Please help me understand. Please fix my leaky roof. Please show me the real holes so they may be repaired. I am tired of moving the buckets around to compensate for the leaks. I don't know how to fix them."

Unworthiness and acceptance are your agreements. These are the sources for all the leaks in your roof. You are spending your life trying to gain acceptance, show your worth, and avoid criticism. You like to be alone because there is no one to criticize or judge you.

"Why do I enjoy activities others view as exhilarating and dangerous? I feel guilty enjoying life, doing activities that make me feel young. Why do I feel the need to play hard!"

Your need for excitement is a function of your desire for freedom. Freedom from all the pressures of acceptance and building worthiness. It is your relief, not an agreement or a sin. This is not selfish. This is life. Live it and enjoy it.

"When work needs to get done, I need to do it now! Why can't it wait until tomorrow? Why does work always come first? Why can't I enjoy my free time, take a weekend off, go on vacations?"

Relaxing does not build worthiness. You began work at an early age. Daytime is for work, not play. You worked to earn money. Money was a sign of your worth. The more money you had, the more proof you were worthy. Your performance was rewarded.

"Do I always have to be in charge? Is that really me? I don't feel like that is me. Do I just not see it?"

You like to be in control when you are comfortable with the task because you can display your worthiness, and you will perform with perfection. You shy away from assuming a position of control if you are not 100 percent confident you can do the job, to avoid criticism.

"If I end up getting divorced, I fear losing all my stuff, especially family keepsakes, memorable furniture from my parents and grandparents. Is this greed?"

Your fear of losing your belongings is not greed as you first thought. It is a fear that the signs of your accomplishments, your worth, will be lost. Greed is the pursuit of riches for riches' sake. Your riches are symbolic, not materialistic.

"Why does everything have to be perfect? Why am I a perfectionist?"

You are a perfectionist simply to leave no room for criticism.

This conversation prompted the following prayer:

"My whole life has been revealed to me today. Today starts the healing. Today is new. Lord, help me feel worthy, accepted, and teach me to appropriately deal with criticism. Help me to feel worthy and accepted in your eyes, so the criticisms and pressures of this world diminish.

"Continue to open my eyes so I may flush out more symptoms and cure my heart. Please deliver me from these negative spirits, Heavenly Father, and fill those former dark spots in my heart with your love. I pray for comfort, peace, and patience as you solidify my house, O Lord. I'll wait for the roof to be fixed as long as the foundation and walls are strong and can sustain the roof."

> ✝ "By wisdom a house is built, and through understanding it is established; through knowledge its rooms are filled with rare and beautiful treasures." (Prov 24:3)

Insight: "That Rock Home…is laid stone by stone, foundations, walls, roof, by the acts of obedience, the daily following of My wishes, the loving doing of My will."[16]

Gaining Wisdom from God-Led Readings

I often questioned my own authority to write a book for God. I have none. I have no formal theological training. My concern was increased by listening to radio sermons and hearing the detail to which scripture is subjected, dissected, and compared to other historical documentation. I find it truly admirable the depth of insight Bible scholars put forth analyzing scripture; acutely skilled researchers, no doubt blessed by God to help explain the Bible.

Without formal training, I was concerned about being scripturally uneducated. I have written what I have heard and expect people to challenge me based on their interpretations of scripture. I'm also convinced the same verse can have different meanings to different people. Interpretations are drawn from people's own beliefs, experiences, knowledge, or needs.

However, this theological debate with myself posed a significant distraction and created doubt in my mind whether I was really pursuing God's purpose for my life. Then God revealed this nonbiblical reference from a random book I was reading and set me straight. It is evident again, how God communicates to us in times of need.

Insight: "God enables you to teach others about Jesus. Though theological training is useful, it is not as important as having a vibrant, living relationship with God, where his Spirit permanently writes on your heart."[17]

Wisdom from the Bible

Any individual line in the Bible can speak directly to us and provide guidance and wisdom. This is how the Bible becomes personal.

I believe it is important to read the Bible in its entirety before attempting to study every verse. After you have read the Bible once, it is much easier to slowly read and digest. I am now familiar enough with the Bible, so when I read a certain verse, I don't worry about the surrounding text or story line. This story illustrates how a simple verse, delivered with perfect timing, can provide the personal wisdom necessary to guide us during our weakest moments and lapses in faith.

* * *

I helped my son with his high school senior project. Given his business orientation and my desire to begin a Christian company to share my learnings on social media, we set up Have Hope 316. We formed the company, set up an accounting system, started a website and Twitter account.

I began updating the Twitter account regularly with God's messages. I started following Christian leaders and felt like I could make a contribution for God online. I posted and retweeted periodically over two years and accumulated a grand total of five followers who were not relatives.

This was one of those times when you realize you're heading down the wrong path. I was disappointed at my number of followers, and no one ever retweeted any of my material. Then God gave me the following message to address my frustration *and* led me to 2 Corinthians 7:4, giving me the confidence to keep trying:

> You trouble yourself over Have Hope 316. Do not be troubled, for your time is not yet here. Continue to lay a strong foundation from which to build. The ultimate success of this project will not be determined by a Facebook page or a Twitter account. It will be dependent upon my blessing. Do your diligence, but stay focused on me. Your purpose is for me to gain followers, not for you to gain followers.

† I have great confidence in you; I take great pride in you. I am greatly encouraged; in all our troubles my joy knows no bounds.
(2 Cor 7:4)

Knowing 2 Corinthians is a letter Paul wrote to the Christians in Corinth nearly two thousand years ago, can we extract this one verse and use it as encouragement from God? Can we accept this as God's Word to each of us? ABSOLUTELY!

It's even more exciting when we are led to a verse that addresses a specific personal question in real time, exactly when we need it the most. In this situation, because of my lackluster Twitter account, I was concerned I was not pursuing God's will, and as a result, I was not receiving his support, so I became discouraged with my entire God effort. Doubt can be a dreadful disease if left untreated.

This is how the Bible evolves from a history lesson to a source of inspiration, guidance, and comfort for each of us individually. There was no question God directed me to this verse. I opened the Bible to this verse, and its message struck me.

Alternatively, you may also search the Bible for answers to specific questions. You might experience divine guidance, which is wonderfully fulfilling, and your answers will be clear.

Be careful not to take your findings out of context by embracing a passage that most closely follows your self-will. Do not use eisegesis to read into the verse whatever you want it to mean. This would be misguided, and possibly even dangerous, and is not the supernatural element I am addressing. Certainly, the Bible can and should be a guide for making personal decisions, but only under the correct pretext.

STEP 10

DISCERNMENT

DISCERNMENT IS THE ABILITY TO distinguish between good and evil, right versus wrong, truth versus fiction. Deciphering the truth can be confusing, particularly when you are in the minority, against popular opinion and clever opposition.

I'm not going to apologize for being forthright when discussing evil or painting an ominous picture of the spiritual realm and ongoing warfare. There is support for spiritual warfare in both Testaments of the Bible.

Although we may never fully understand the spirit world, heaven and hell, Satan, angels, and good and evil influences in today's world, mere awareness may save us. These topics should be brought to the surface and discussed. I'm not afraid to oblige.

We cannot control Satan. Satan will be Satan. Fortunately, as our discernment improves with spiritual maturity, we recognize Satan's handiwork and can avoid his schemes. God brings clarity to those who seek it.

Do not blame God when someone chooses evil over good. God allows our free will, and there are ungodly people in the world, so evil happens. But your God-led discernment can prevent you from becoming one of those people.

If not for spiritual guidance, what drives our daily decisions? The needs of the flesh and the wants of the self. What your flesh thinks is good, might not be good at this time. If everyone operated by the wants of their own self, conflicts and stresses would surely arise!

Avoid Hell, but Not the Topic

Do not avoid the topic of hell as many do. Hell is real. Hell is not a warning. Hell is too late. I will not be accessible to those in hell.

Do not fear hell, for hell is conquered in my name. Fear for the people without this knowledge.

I am in complete control of my creation, but Satan has limited abilities. You must understand this foe. What are his strengths and weaknesses? What other forces make this opposition dangerous?

Spiritual Warfare

Satan is aware of your spiritual progress. He delights in confusion, distractions, and false messages. He wants you to believe you are not worthy of my love, forgiveness, and communication. He preys on people's insecurities. He wants you to feel condemned and hopeless. He wants you to feel time pressure. He wants you to feel uncomfortable, lonely, lost.

You are not lost. You will always have my compassion, my attention when you need it. Hear my comforting voice. Rebuke the devil when you hear his voice. Close the door of your heart, spirit, mind, and soul to the evil one in my name, and he will be gone. Believe him away.

Be secure in me, my child. Gain strength from my power and love. Be confident and strong against the devil, for I am with you. Put him in his place with confidence. He will fail. He is nothing but a deceitful liar. I have defeated him. He is a coward before me. He is powerless against me. I am the almighty God. He is a fallen angel.

Identifying and Battling Agreements

Agreements are either willingly or unknowingly made with Satan. They are concessions you make. You surrender to a feeling Satan has imposed. This gives Satan a foothold for the future until you acknowledge the agreement and renounce it in the name of Jesus Christ.

Do not concede to a task because it is made too difficult by Satan. Do not let him win even once. Do not make any compromises, especially when you recognize Satan's involvement. Fight back in the name of Jesus Christ, and Satan will retreat. You will quickly feel the relief.

Agreements bind the heart and spirit. They may be subtle, but they give Satan an opening from which to work on, to grab ahold, to expose. Pray for these agreements to be revealed. If you knew what they were or how they came about, you would not have made them. Agreements made in your lifetime, regardless of how early or late in life, form the source of a leak in your roof.

Do not be afraid to break these agreements. Do not fear what you may learn or suffer to cleanse yourself. These agreements are not good. They are evil. You were deceived, and now you will see. You need to fight back to regain the part of your heart that was stolen from you.

Do not be ashamed you have made these agreements for you did not know; you could not know. Your heart is happy for this revelation, for it is a step toward further healing.

Cleanse your heart of these compromises, of these defeats, of these feelings of unworthiness you have conceded to. Forgive all participants in your agreements so you may put your past behind you.

Going forward, recognize when an agreement is being presented. When you find yourself giving in to a feeling or action you know in your heart is negative, ungodly, against my loving nature, resist!

Fight Fire with Fire

† "You, dear children, are from God and have overcome them, because the one who is in you is greater than he who is in the world." (1 John 4:4)

There will always be bumps in the road, setbacks generally caused by your own free will or by Satan affecting you or your surroundings. He is the master manipulator. He succeeds when you do not recognize him. In all you hear, experience, or witness, consider the source.

When facing difficulty in discernment or with a decision, pray. Sometimes a quick answer may appear obvious, but beware, this could be Satan's way of forcing a bad decision or reaction by creating a false sense of urgency. Be leery of unnecessary time pressure. Be cautious of reacting without praying. If it is my will, I will create the time for an appropriate response.

Do not wear down or doubt. Instead of giving up out of resignation, step out and say, "This one's yours, Lord, take care of it, please. I have faith and will trust you."

You win the war through persistence. Maintain your commitment, and the opposition will eventually subside, leading to a much freer opportunity for us to grow. Keep the faith and pray for strength.

When your distractions are great, so must be your fight! You cannot overcome unusual circumstances with usual behavior. Recognize your situation and attack with fervor. Do not lie down and accept defeat.

Satan wins when you accept defeat. When you say, "I have no inspiration," Satan wins. Fight fire with fire. You have the tools to win every time. Use them until you win. You have the power in Jesus.

Mental and Physical Well-Being

Mental tiredness can bring down the energy of the physical body, and physical tiredness weakens your mental capacity. Just as physical exercise requires periods of rest, mental rest is also essential to maintain spiritual growth. This balance keeps your body in check.

It is much harder to concentrate, stay focused, and defeat temptation when you are physically tired. You become lazy. When the flesh is weak, the spirit tends to follow, and concentration and willpower suffer. You cannot grow weak in your battle against evil. You cannot let your guard down, or your discernment will become blurred, and you will expose yourselves to deception.

Keep your mind and body clean and well-rested. Be careful what you put into your body, for it affects both your physical and mental well-being.

Temptations

As long as you have free will, you must choose between doing good and doing evil.

Many temptations present themselves to dare you. Dare you to be someone you are not, to do something you would not otherwise do, to fulfill a desire for risk, excitement, or other earthly pleasures.

Temptation is clever, customized to each individual according to his or her own personality and weaknesses. Satan knows how to get your attention!

Let go and feel my guidance, my urging, your inner voice giving you advice. Listen and decipher the source. Does the urge cause you peace or stress? What are the motivations for the actions? Are you doing this for yourself or for others? Does the urge or action bring glory to me? Temptation from the evil one is easy to identify when you ask yourself, "Would this be pleasing to God?"

I bind the spirits of the evil one. As I do, your temptations will lessen. You may wonder, "Why don't I feel like doing this or that?" You will be comfortable with who you are. It is because the particular temptation has been bound. The temptations will still exist, still present themselves, but they will not interest you, and will not be tempting any longer.

DISCERNMENT— PERSONAL REFLECTION

† "You believe that there is one God. Good! Even the demons believe that—and shudder." (James 2:19)

Discernment Defined

Discernment is simply the ability to judge whether something is good and godly, or evil. I believe there is a lot of confusion over what is right and wrong in the world today. The more we know about the opposition, the more prepared we are to recognize evil and resist. You will face situations that require proper discernment in your journey. God will provide the warning signs that will allow you to identify and avoid the danger.

Satan's Résumé

The name of Satan is well known, but people hold different views on Satan's role and even his mere existence in the world. As Christians, we rely on what the Bible says about Satan. The Bible is clear: Satan is real. He is God's adversary, and therefore our adversary. We find the means to protect ourselves against Satan, his authorities, and demons in the Bible.

† "Be self-controlled and alert. Your enemy the devil prowls around like a roaring lion looking for someone to devour." (1 Pet 5:8)

† "Put on the full armor of God so that you can take a stand against the devil's schemes. For our struggle is not against flesh and blood, but against the rulers, against the authorities, against the powers of this dark world and against the spiritual forces of evil in the heavenly realms." (Eph 6:11–12)

† "But the Lord is faithful, and he will strengthen and protect you from the evil one." (2 Thess 3:3)

You may ask, "Why spend time writing about Satan?"

Because, if it were not for Satan, our relationship with God would be much different today. In Genesis 3, the serpent (revealed later in the Bible as Satan), deceived Adam and Eve, enticing them to eat from the forbidden tree, telling Eve that eating the fruit of the tree would cause their "eyes to be opened and they would be like God, knowing good from evil."

Prior to this deception, Adam and Eve shared a personal relationship with God, depicted here as God meets Adam and Eve in the Garden of Eden:

† "Then the man and his wife heard the sound of the Lord God as he was walking in the garden in the cool of the day, and they hid from the Lord God among the trees of the garden." (Gen 3:8)

It does not appear Adam and Eve were shocked to find God in the garden, as this was not the first time. However, this time they hid themselves because they were ashamed.

Eating the forbidden fruit changed their relationship with God forever. They were deceived, became disobedient, and ultimately were distanced from God, not drawn closer as the serpent promised. Similarly, we learn in the book of Isaiah, Satan's desire to be like God, or better than God, caused his ejection from heaven.

We have the advantage of knowing Satan exists, and we know his history—knowledge that might have been helpful for Adam and Eve. Satan was originally an angel of God. When God cast Satan out of heaven, one-third of the angels of heaven followed him, and two-thirds remained with God. As a fan of God, I like those odds.

Many references are made to the serpent and Satan in both the Old and New Testament. But the connection is not specifically revealed until the final book of the Bible, Revelation:

† "And there was war in heaven. Michael and his angels fought against the dragon, and the dragon and his angels fought back. But he was not strong enough, and they lost their place in heaven. The great dragon was hurled down—that ancient serpent called the devil, or Satan, who leads the whole world astray. He was hurled to the earth, and his angels with him." (Rev 12:7–9)

Satan Has Not Retired

Until the end-times, we must remain steadfast in our focus on God and resist the temptations Satan creates. Satan afflicted Job in an unsuccessful effort to turn him away from God. He unsuccessfully tempted Jesus. To think Satan is no longer deceiving people today is foolish. He hasn't retired.

There are modern-day stories of God's miracles, encounters with heaven from near-death experiences and other purported divine events. Likewise, there are many accounts of Satan's influence in today's society. Much is written about this evil, and I would encourage your research, but allow God to provide the clarity and discernment between what is fiction and nonfiction.

Satan is a master at disguising his influence. The less you know about his tactics, the easier it is for him to deceive the world.

Unlike God, Satan is neither omnipotent nor omniscient. He can only be in one place at a time, and neither Satan nor his demons can read your thoughts. With this knowledge, be aware what you say out loud, including your prayers, is fair game for Satan to hear. Prayers in silence are strictly between you and God.

Christians are disrupters of Satan's kingdom. As you grow in spiritual maturity, your visibility to Satan increases and you attract his attention. If you interfere with his kingdom, you become an important target.

We will focus on battling deception and temptation. This war can be won every time because we have faith in Jesus Christ. Jesus is already the victor. Satan is no match for Jesus. Demons withdraw at the mention of Jesus Christ.

Reread the Psalms. Replace David's woes with spiritual warfare. Now you can relate to the fear, modern-day evil, and hell. The Psalms will become twice as powerful.

Hell Is Too Late!

> † "Therefore let everyone who is godly pray to you *while you may be found; surely when the mighty waters rise, they will not reach him.*" (Ps 32:6)

There appears to come a time when God cannot be found—in hell. God's message reads, "Hell is too late. God will not be accessible to those in hell."

There is no rescue from hell, no second chances. Hell is not God's punishment; hell is for those who choose hell (they choose to be separated from God). Everyone has a choice. Choose to believe in God.

I know people who believe in God but not Satan and hell. One of my best friends had a near-death experience as a child. He dove into the deep end of a swimming pool without knowing how to swim! He found himself entering a long, blinding white tunnel before being rescued from the pool and revived. He believes in God and the afterlife but not in hell. The Bible is clear; hell and spiritual warfare exist.

- "On the wicked he will rain fiery coals and burning sulfur; a scorching wind will be their lot." (Ps 11:6)

- "Do not be afraid of those who kill the body but cannot kill the soul. Rather, be afraid of the One who can destroy both soul and body in hell." (Matt 10:28)

Good Guys Finish Last

Ever hear the saying, "Good guys finish last?"

I find myself in this position often. In business, this can be painfully true and frustrating. I know several business leaders who do not operate ethically. They are ruthless toward employees and customers and will do anything to earn a dollar. They thrive.

I often wonder what happened to "What goes around comes around." Some people seem to be immune. The ruthless become wealthy and successful because the temptation of power and status on earth outweigh the perceived benefits of godly obedience, and they have the support of the great deceiver.

I take comfort in Psalm 10 that I am not alone in this observation, and apparently, this has been going on for some time!

- "In his arrogance the wicked man hunts down the weak, who are caught in the schemes he devises.
"He boasts of the cravings of his heart; he blesses the greedy and reviles the Lord.
"In his pride the wicked man does not seek him; in all his thoughts there is no room for God.
"His ways are always prosperous; he is haughty and your laws are far from him; he sneers at all his enemies." (Ps 10:2–5)

Satan delights in evil and rewards ungodliness. We can take comfort that evil will ultimately be punished and the righteous will be elevated. But I wouldn't mind a win every now and then!

I had a brief exchange with God about Satan. He quickly answered and gave biblical support:

"Is it possible the devil is prompting me to pray out loud so he can hear me and know my desires? For otherwise, he will not know. Is it okay to pray in silence?"

> † "But when you pray, go into your room, close the door and pray to your Father, who is unseen. Then your Father, who sees what is done in secret will reward you." (Matt 6:6)

* * *

"Why does it seem like the wicked thrive?"
The day of reckoning will come.

> † "The Lord is known by his justice; the wicked are ensnared by the work of their hands. The wicked return to the grave, all the nations that forget God." (Ps 9:16–17)

* * *

"You created the heavens, the earth, sky, sun, moon, stars, and every living thing. Why don't you destroy Satan?"
In Satan's place will come another.

* * *

"How will this be different when Jesus returns?"
Ultimately, God will prevail, and Satan will be doomed to hell. Trust that the wicked will be defeated.

† "God is just: He will pay back trouble to those who trouble you and give relief to you who are troubled, and to us as well. This will happen when the Lord Jesus is revealed from heaven in blazing fire with his powerful angels. He will punish those who do not know God and do not obey the gospel of our Lord Jesus." (2 Thess 1:6–8)

† "And the devil, who deceived them, was thrown into the lake of burning sulfur, where the beast and the false prophet had been thrown. They will be tormented day and night for ever and ever." (Rev 20:10)

Jesus Who?

It is challenging for a young Christian to avoid distractions and progress through the stages of spiritual maturity. I looked for every advantage I could get. I felt my fight would be easier if I prayed silently, so Satan would not know my innermost desires and concerns. I wanted to remain stealthy to stay off Satan's radar. (In the back of my mind, though, I always felt I gave myself away through my writings anyway.)

Finally, one morning, combating a flurry of obstacles, I prayed out loud, thinking I was commanding Satan to leave me alone:

"Satan, be gone. In the name of Jesus, be gone. I close the door of my heart, mind, and spirit upon all thoughts, noises, and distractions except the word of God."

And I immediately heard in my mind, **"Jesus who?"**

I was shocked. This was completely different than the calming messages I hear from God. This was a mean, curt, accusing attack. Suddenly, spiritual opposition became extraordinarily real and personal. I was momentarily gripped with fear, but the Holy Spirit immediately inspired this prayer:

"In the name of Jesus Christ, devil of fear get out of me now! I pray for the fire of the Holy Spirit, the Spirit of God to destroy this devil of fear. Fill me with your love, O Christ of God, and surround me with your protection."

This spontaneous response by the Holy Spirit was authoritative, a clear demonstration of God's protection. It was literally instantaneous. These words came out of my mouth before I could think.

I experienced a small bout of spiritual warfare in my little bedroom. I would never have foreseen this occurring in the sanctity of my home. I was a spectator, witnessing the supernatural exchange.

Can we truly be stealthy in the presence of evil? I prefer to trust the omnipotent God and let him fight this war for me.

The Witch?

Temptation is not always obvious. That is why astute discernment is necessary to protect us against clever attempts to derail our faith.

During my brief period of bachelorhood, I entertained an out-of-town colleague one weekday night. We went to dinner at a local pub and had some male bonding time, then stayed far into the night for drinks. As the evening began to wind down, we played darts with a young woman and her friend in the gaming area.

I don't remember much about the friend, but I eventually exchanged phone numbers with the young woman named Vicky. She was attractive but mysterious in a way I could not explain. There was a physical and intellectual attraction, but also some sort of spiritual connection.

We were unusually comfortable with each other, considering we just met. Our conversation was engaging. It was way out of my character to exchange phone numbers; much too aggressive for me. But I wanted to see Vicky again.

After dropping my colleague at his hotel, I proceeded to text Vicky, and we met at a local breakfast spot. It was early morning.

She was now with a different friend who was unique in appearance, many tattoos and piercings. This new person appeared much rougher and less personable than the friend from the bar. Vicky was also a little more serious.

It was strange she was meeting a friend at two o'clock in the morning as if they were preparing to get their night started.

The conversation turned quickly to religion. Vicky told me she was ordained. She asked if I would ever be open to an alternative view of religion, some sort of twist on traditional Christianity?

Vicky left alone for the ladies' room. Upon returning, she responded she "was not supposed to tell me anything more at this time." I felt like she was disappointed and wanted to continue, but was heeding someone's advice to be silent.

She said I had an unusual aura about me, like a blanket of protection she could not penetrate. She was a little confused by it.

She said, "I'm usually pretty good about sizing people up, but for some reason, I'm not able to get a good read of you."

We parted shortly thereafter, but I was determined to learn more about her.

The next time we met, religion overtook the conversation. I began to sense we did not share the same views about God. She was more about nature; I was more about Jesus. I gave her the book that triggered my transition from awareness to acceptance, Rebecca Brown's *He Came to Set the Captives Free*.

Vicky said her friends thought she was a witch. I wasn't totally surprised. We spent a lot of time that night in deep religious conversation. She told me which musicians I should avoid as she perused my CD collection. There was more spirituality to her than I originally thought! I was very intrigued.

Our final encounter began with Vicky returning my book, stating she could not read it; she felt the need to "rebuke the book."

Huh?

On our way to dinner, she again approached the topic of an alternative to the traditional Christian mindset. There is not one omnipotent God, but God is everywhere in nature. I felt like, if I agreed to this concept, she would continue to stretch me further and further from my faith with each discussion, until I lost sight of my original core belief.

Our friendship ended after a couple of weeks, with a lot of questions still unanswered in my mind. I was well into my transformation at this point and aware of the concept of spiritual warfare, but I had never been tested like this, in real human form.

Weeks later, I heard from a friend that the ordained temptress was interpreting dreams on a local radio station.

Certainly, I am in a much better place now because of my discernment. Had we continued seeing each other, I'm pretty sure I would not be writing a book about having a relationship with God. I am certain the blanket of protection Vicky sensed was provided by God.

This entire experience was a test by the devil, albeit not a difficult one. I escaped by the grace of God. It demonstrates how Satan can tailor a temptation to our unique, personal weaknesses.

We must embrace the concept of discernment, acknowledge that spiritual warfare exists, and trust God to reveal the truth.

I have always felt protected. I have done many irresponsible things in my life that easily could have ended badly. I have faith in the spirits God sends to keep us safe. I never forget the lessons of Rebecca Brown's book.

My experience with Vicky was mild compared to stories I've read about people becoming entangled with evil. Was she a real witch? I'll never know. She seemed harmless enough. That's the kind of unsuspecting temptation that could have sidetracked my faith forever.

† "But you are a shield around me, O Lord, you bestow glory on me and lift up my head." (Ps 3:3)

† "But let all who take refuge in you be glad; let them ever sing for joy. Spread your protection over them, that those who love your name may rejoice in you." (Ps 5:11)

Satan Can Go to Hell

† "But the cowardly, the unbelieving, the vile, the murderers, the sexually immoral, those who practice magic arts, the idolaters and all liars—their place will be in the fiery lake of burning sulfur." (Rev 21:8a)

I'm convinced Satan influences some areas of the world more powerfully than others; parts of the world where sin, prostitution, and crime are openly prevalent. More subtle signs include the lack of simple human decency and respect, which seems to worsen with every generation.

Is this continued degradation of human behavior evidence of Satan's progress? Has every generation felt like they lost ground to evil? If so, when does it end?

The Bible describes an end-time event, referred to as the rapture, when all Christian believers will simultaneously rise and join Jesus Christ in heaven.

† "For the Lord himself will come down from heaven, with a loud command, with the voice of the archangel and with the trumpet call of God, and the dead in Christ will rise first. After that, we who are still alive and are left will be caught up together with them in the clouds to meet the Lord in the air. And so we will be with the Lord forever." (1 Thess 4:16–17)

Following the rapture, the ungodly will torment the earth for seven years until they are defeated by the second coming of Jesus.

But what can we do now? Must we concede to society's moral deterioration? Do we merely hold on until we hear the trumpet?

No, there is plenty of good in this world! We must be bold in our spiritual fight, not cower to the pressures of the misdirected. Who is more committed to their cause, good or evil?

Spiritual warfare is real and frightening and sounds like *Star Wars*-type material to many. This is how Satan wants it. The less believable, the more stealthily he can operate.

One of my favorite books is *Listen, the Lord*, as you may note from the "Insight" quotes throughout this book. *Listen, the Lord* contends to be written by seven spiritual listeners relaying messages from Jesus. Of course, this is possible, and the material in the book has been very supportive and comforting. One passage specifically outlines a process for combating and casting out evil:

Insight: "I would have you use four steps in the casting out of evil. Never omit one.

First, be still and when you feel My Power strong within you, command the evil to come forth, as I did on earth—but command in My Name.

Second, pray that the fire of My Spirit destroy that evil. Some of My workers hesitate to ask Me to destroy evil. It is My will that you do so.

Third, pray that My Love fill the empty one to overflowing.

Fourth, ask for the light of My Protection..."[18]

Is it entirely necessary to believe there is a fiery furnace in the underground? Maybe not. Can we comprehend heaven exactly? Not at all. But heaven and hell are both discussed in the Bible! Therefore, we should acknowledge Satan exists and accept there is a means to eternally reward the righteous and punish the wicked.

Evil Tactics

† "Watch out for false prophets. They come to you in sheep's clothing, but inwardly they are ferocious wolves." (Matt 7:15)

† "And no wonder for Satan himself masquerades as an angel of light." (2 Cor 11:14)

It's important to understand the purpose, strength, and tactics of the opposition to make sure we are not deceived into thinking we are winning, when instead, we may be on the path to defeat!

In my mother's testimony from the chapter on acceptance, there was a period when she attended church, and at the same time, believed in reincarnation. Outside of church, she openly discussed those beliefs with anyone who would listen.

Had she not been converted, this could have been an example of how Satan can infiltrate Christianity in a fearfully subtle and inconspicuous way with an alternative, deceitful message.

You would think churches would be safe havens for Christians, but on the contrary, they are Satan's greatest targets!

Heavenly Support

> ✝ "In the same way, I tell you, there is rejoicing in the presence of the angels of God over one sinner who repents." (Luke 15:10)

Let's end this chapter on a high note! There are other supernatural beings operating in the spiritual realm. Let's talk about angels, God's spiritual secret service. The Bible specifically names two angels, Gabriel and Michael.

Gabriel is a messenger of God and is the most frequently mentioned angel. His name means "God is my strength." He helps Daniel in the Old Testament and announces good news to Elizabeth and Mary in the New Testament.

> ✝ "And I heard a man's voice from Ulai calling, 'Gabriel, tell this man the meaning of the vision.'" (Dan 8:16)

> ✝ "While I was speaking and praying…Gabriel, the man I had seen in the earlier vision, came to me in swift flight about the time of the evening sacrifice." (Dan 9:20–21)

✝ "The angel answered, 'I am Gabriel. I stand in the presence of God, and I have been sent to speak to you and to tell you this good news.'" (Luke 1:19)

✝ "In the sixth month, God sent the angel Gabriel to Nazareth, a town in Galilee, to a virgin pledged to be married to a man named Joseph, a descendant of David. The virgin's name was Mary." (Luke 1:26–27)

The archangel Michael is a warrior, one of many chief princes among God's angels. He saved Daniel in the Old Testament and will lead God's army of angels against Satan in the end-time battle with Satan's forces.

✝ "But the prince of the Persian kingdom resisted me twenty-one days. Then Michael, one of the chief princes, came to help me, because I was detained there with the king of Persia [Satan]." (Dan 10:13)

✝ "At that time Michael, the great prince who protects your people, will arise. There will be a time of distress such as has not happened from the beginning of nations until then. But at that time your people—everyone whose name is found written in the book—will be delivered." (Dan 12:1)

✝ "And there was war in heaven. Michael and his angels fought against the dragon, and the dragon and his angels fought back. But he [Satan] was not strong enough, and they lost their place in heaven." (Rev 12:7–8)

There is also an angel of the Lord mentioned in the Old Testament, whose name is never revealed, and who is not mentioned in the New Testament. Many believe this angel was the preincarnate Jesus, or perhaps the presence of God.

† "As the flame blazed up from the altar toward heaven, the angel of the Lord ascended in the flame. When the angel of the Lord did not show himself again to Manoah and his wife, Manoah realized that it was the angel of the Lord." (Judg 13:20a–21)

The most common angels are called ministering angels or spirits. There are also protective angels, who formed a hedge of protection around Job:

† "Have you not put a hedge around him and his household and everything he has?" (Job 1:10a)

Clearly, God and his angels are superior; *they* did the casting out. We are no match for Satan without God. Not only does the blood of Jesus protect us, but we also have the power of the blood of Jesus.

Thank you, Lord Jesus, for your power, mercy, grace, forgiveness, comfort, joy, guidance, strength, love, patience, understanding, sense of humor, and confidence.

God in Us

This section is conjecture because, once again, we cannot understand God's ways. But throughout God's lessons, we often hear God is with us always. We are filled with the Holy Spirit. The Bible supports this claim multiple times.

† "And if the Spirit of him who raised Jesus from the dead is living in you, he who raised Christ from the dead will also give life to your mortal bodies through his Spirit, who lives in you." (Rom 8:11)

† "Don't you know that you yourselves are God's temple and that God's Spirit lives in you?" (1 Cor 3:16)

The message appears straightforward; God lives in us. We've already learned humans can be demon-possessed. Jesus called out demons by their names. So why can't we also be God-possessed?

Maybe the spiritual battlefield is not in our minds, but somehow in our beings. A spiritual battle between the Holy Spirit and demons within us. The victor is determined by our own free will, whether we demonstrate proper discernment and are obedient, or we ignore the urges of the Holy Spirit and drift to evil. Both good and evil exist, but their prominence is decided by our desires and actions.

> Look inside yourself. This is where I am. It is difficult to grasp this concept. I'm not just with you during quiet time, but all day, every day. We are together.
>
> You have written this many times but have never internalized it.
>
> I know what you did, what's in your heart, the hairs on your head, your real intent. I am also the God of the universe.
>
> How is this possible? Because I am in you.

I am not sure why, after all these years, I have not taken this literally. I believed God was with us remotely, yet he somehow knew everything about us. It certainly seems more plausible he is in us, even though we can't explain how.

This is a wonderful and scary proposition. But one which appears hard to deny when we open ourselves to the possibility.

    We spend more time in devotion with God.
        His Spirit grows with us.
            Evil is minimized.
                We become pure from within.
                    We receive discernment to combat temptation.
                    Our lives are transformed.

STEP 11

FULFILLMENT OF PURPOSE

✝ "However, as it is written, 'No eye has seen, no ear has heard, no mind has conceived what God has prepared for those who love him'—but God has revealed it to us by his Spirit." (1 Cor 2:9–10)

The Path Traveled

Your self-will is improving every day. You are consistently finding time to be with me. You are more patient. You are more accurately discerning good from evil.

You seek wisdom. You read and embrace the Bible. You read other inspirational books and practice the lessons learned. You listen to Christian music. You keep journals. You kneel.

You recognize my authority and my love. You do not question the source of your messages or our ability to communicate. You enjoy the experience. It brings you joy. It lifts your spirit.

You are growing in me. The people around you are growing in me. You are making a difference in many people's lives, some of whom you do not know.

You have planted many seeds, and some will grow. You act boldly in faith, and I will reward you. I know you cannot believe your own ears talking about your experiences.

You are bold. Everything about you is bold—your heart, passion, enthusiasm. Pray for your life to be magnified through my love, set apart from the world, glorified in my name. Do not fear the recognition of being bold in my name.

Transition Time

When does a child become a man? Does a man ever not also feel like a child? When does the student become a teacher?

There comes a time when the child begins to think like a man, and slowly gains the confidence to act like a man and do manly activities. At the beginning of this journey, you were a child. Today you are a man, full of wisdom and filled with the Holy Spirit.

You are beginning to lay the foundation for your testimony with those around you. You believe I will lead you, and I believe you will lead others.

You have gone from the intensity of learning to the intensity of life. It is time to demonstrate what you know. I have given you a gift, which must not be wasted. I will fill your heart with courage and initiative. Channel your energy towards my works.

You need to overcome your inhibitions, your insecurities. Trust me to give you the strength and the knowledge to perform my will. Trust me to consider all the feelings in your heart, all your abilities, all you are capable of, and all you are not. I may challenge you, but it will not seem overbearing.

You read the Truth, know the Truth, and live the Truth. Now it is time to share the Truth.

God the Coach

Coaches have players who start the game. Teams also have bench players, minor league players, and practice squads. The coach knows best when a player is ready to succeed at the job. All players want to play, but they are not objective in their own self-evaluation. Coaches are needed to evaluate and develop their players so they will succeed when asked to perform!

Players learn the playbook and learn their role on the team. They learn about the opposition, its strengths and tactics. They gain experience, endurance, and confidence by practicing.

The coach begins by inserting his inexperienced players sparingly in situations appropriate for young players' developmental maturity. They play, learn from their experience, and wait for the next game; honing their skills, anxious to play again.

Be patient. The coach knows you want to play and knows what is best for you and the team.

You Are Wanted

I chose you for a reason. You are not perfect, and people who know you know this. As a result, I have a greater opportunity to demonstrate my power and love. The changes in you will be more obvious and compelling to those who hear you witness.

Your words are powerful because you speak the truth, so people will appreciate your insight.

I am giving you the tools to be a teacher, not a preacher. You are a teacher of business every day. I will make you a teacher of Jesus.

Trust I will not waste your desire to do works for me. Few have your desire. Be patient, for you do not know what lies ahead. We look at life from different perspectives. You, from the present, because that is all you know, and I, from the future, because I can.

Do not be obsessed with theology; that would be a waste of your talents. People who need help are not interested in your educational background or theological training. They are interested in your love and willingness to help. In some cases, extensive schooling is necessary because there is no intimacy with me.

Learn of me with your heart and not your mind. Teach from your heart and not your mind.

> † "When they saw the courage of Peter and John and realized that they were unschooled, ordinary men, they were astonished and they took note that these men had been with Jesus." (Acts 4:13)

Go Forth

Your courage to witness will increase with practice, over time. Begin by witnessing with folks of similar beliefs, sharing stories of faith. Your confidence will grow with each conversation. They will confirm my Truth. You will feed off this interaction, and it will make you strong. You will need this experiential foundation when you witness to the rest of the world. This will happen in my time, naturally, when you are ready.

You are now equipped to interact with others. It would have been permanently discouraging for you to attempt this unarmed. You have the confidence through your experiences and your newfound faith to step out of your quiet room.

You will receive, and you will give. Spiritual discussions build awareness. Some people will want to hear more, others will not.

Share with your family. It is important for them to know what you are doing spiritually and that you are fulfilling your purpose.

Show signs of your renewed faith during the day. Your spirit will be lifted by this sharing. You will be respected for your display, and it will provide leadership and direction for others.

Your witnessing will make people aware of me. This is all I can ask. You may not see any changes in the people you witness to, but I do.

Demonstrate What You Know

You want a plan for your ministry? Develop it! Research and get started. Have you grown weak in your initiative? Take action and quit waiting for others. I can guide your work, but you still must do the work. Prayers will seemingly go unanswered if you do not perform accompanying required works.

Who learns to swim without getting wet? You learn much more from diving into the water than you do from sitting on the side of the pool watching. Who learns how to ride a bike without hopping on? You must get on the bike and begin pedaling before you move anywhere.

Do not let your current capabilities limit your vision. My capabilities are limitless; therefore, yours are too. You don't have to understand, simply believe and try. You only know what you are capable of knowing and do what you are capable of doing. Moses parted the Red Sea, not from his own understanding.

Start by Displaying Your Belief

It is not what you know, but what you do that counts. Everyone is Christian-like in church, but after they leave the church, they clam up. What are you doing? Do you demonstrate my love? My compassion? Are your actions a true reflection of me and what I represent? How do you display your Christianity? Do people know you are a Christian? Are you setting an example or sitting on the sidelines watching?

A high percentage of people have no religion in their life. They do not go to church, and they see no signs of Christian behavior in their everyday lives. How many people do you know who display their Christianity outwardly? How many of your friends or fellow employees go to church regularly, or talk about their belief in me?

You want to do my work? You must first show me you can handle it. It is certainly easier to preach to the choir than it is to preach on the street, but preaching on the street brings people in to listen to the choir.

Testify Wisely

Stay humble during your spiritual advancement. This is not a talent; this is my gift to you.

Encourage others. Be a servant. Do not serve yourself.

Do not decide to testify based on the gain or loss of money.

If you feel like you are trying too hard to accomplish my task, then you are trying too hard. You are missing the mark. Allow me to guide you. I ask you to cooperate and not coordinate.

Deliver a clear message. Do not oversell. No need to oversell a message that has a strong foundation of truth.

All people are different, and your ways are not the same as everyone else's. People interpret messages differently to satisfy their own circumstances. I will work in people's lives and nurture their understanding, but I must get their attention first. Please help me get their attention.

Those needing encouragement the most are the ones beginning the journey. They have questions and doubts and no experiences to draw from. They have no direction, no confidence, no momentum. Give them encouragement! Every Christian started somewhere, sometime, and was helped by someone along the way.

Substance Over Form

My message is delivered in many ways and is received just as effectively by those in need. Do not judge or criticize the delivery method or the recipient. In all situations, people receive my blessings because of their faith, not because of the quality or the method of delivery.

Come away with this: Do not prejudge the impact your message may have on your audience, in whatever form. Do not hesitate to witness on my behalf because the situation may not meet your expectation. Use the opportunity I have given you, without filtering it through your perfectionist standards.

Write from your heart. Do not assume your audience's spiritual level of development. Even mature Christians appreciate the comradery and reinforcement of their beliefs. Everyone is searching. Rest assured, no one has all the answers!

Lessons can be more universally accepted when they speak in general terms. The more general your presentation, the broader the audience. A message can touch the hearts of a thousand people in a thousand different ways. I will fill in the blanks and make it perfectly relevant for each listener. This is my job, not yours. What's most important is that my kingdom is advanced in those who hear.

Anointing

An anointing is a blessing from me. The anointing is present when you call on the name of Jesus. "This I pray in the name of your son, Jesus Christ."

If a project has been anointed, it is blessed for a limited time. If the project is not acted upon, circumstances change, and so does the anointing. Do not procrastinate yourself out of a gift from God. Trust the feeling of anointing.

If you give your child permission to go to the movies this Friday, this does not automatically mean he also has your blessing for the following Friday. If he chooses not to go to the movies with his blessing from you, he must wait until he receives permission again. Circumstances may change during the week, which may affect your decision to bless or not to bless.

My anointing is not only a blessing on a project but the promise of my presence and guidance with the project. Go forth with my anointing and know I am with you.

If you feel obligated to do something for me, but it doesn't feel right, don't do it. Learn to discern the callings. It is not I who creates meaningless busyness or routine in my name. I don't need routine from you. I get enough routine. Routine is stagnant. Routine is neutral—no growth. You go nowhere in neutral.

You will feel comfort when you hear a decision I suggest or support. If you are not confident, continue to pray on the matter until you are confident. Many times, your self-will interferes with your hearing. I am not indecisive. My message will be clear. Your acceptance of my message may be murky.

The Patience of a Butterfly

I could show you my full design for your life, but you'd be determined to achieve it on your own time and not mine. A caterpillar must spend the entire metamorphic period in a cocoon and instinctively emerge when it is fully developed. The time is not wasted, although it appears to be dormant. The caterpillar is just preparing itself for its beautiful reveal. The butterfly does nothing except wait and allow me to work my miracle of transformation.

Know the timing for everything is in my hands, my perfect timing, for those who believe and are willing to put my timing ahead of their own. I know it is difficult to have patience, but emerging too early could be deadly.

FULFILLMENT OF PURPOSE — PERSONAL REFLECTION

† "Commit to the Lord whatever you do, and your plans will succeed." (Prov 16:3)

† "Do not neglect your gift which was given you through…when the body of elders laid their hands on you." (1 Tim 4:14)

GOD CALLS US TO SERVE in different ways, based on our talents, desires, and circumstances. He places us in situations, presents opportunities to witness, and gives us the tools to succeed. Whether we accept to fulfill the calling is a matter of choice.

The pinnacle of our relationship with God is to serve him by fulfilling his purpose for our life. Finding God's will for our life is difficult. We must differentiate between our will to do something for God and God's will for us.

We may not feel we are ready to fulfill God's purpose for our lives. But if God has shared his will, then trust he will also provide the means to carry it out. Have the faith to follow his guidance, or you may lose his support.

Insight: "…one act of surrender to self-will when you know My Will, opens the door to Satan—opens it wide."[19]

Insight: "The ability to know My Will disappears if you do not follow My Will when you know it."[20]

Pray about your reservations. Do not let your hesitations stop you from pursuing God's will. Stay close with God, and he will bridge your confidence gap and provide the assurance you need to continue the journey.

These are some excerpts from my journal, which clearly demonstrate my confusion.

* * *

I have wondered about my purpose to serve God. Writing a book and promoting the path to fulfilling God's purpose would be a worthy accomplishment and would glorify God. So why do I even doubt the calling? Probably because I am completely incapable of doing it on my own.

* * *

I am disappointed and frustrated at my lack of progress toward what I feel is a calling. Have I misunderstood? Is this vision for my personal benefit and not God's will?

* * *

Could it be God has allowed me to start a book and get frustrated, so I get it out of my system and question down the road, "Man, if I had only written a book"? Maybe it's not about the book at all, but about the teachings, to be used some other way?

* * *

I prayed for God to bring purpose to my life. Has he been waiting for me to pray for his purpose to be revealed? Because I feel a sense of certainty I haven't felt before. I now realize God is with me, guiding me, rather than at a distance, telling me what to do. I have gained the confidence to go public and share my story.

Go Vertical and Horizontal

Throughout these lessons, I have emphasized the progressive development of intimacy with God, up to and including ultimately fulfilling his purpose for our lives. I concentrate primarily on describing the means for a vertical relationship, in other words, one-on-one with God.

But God's intention is clearly for us to do more, to share the fruits of this personal relationship with others. He wants us to witness horizontally through works.

Jesus says in Matthew 25:35–36, "For I was hungry and you gave me something to eat, I was thirsty and you gave me something to drink, I was a stranger and you invited me in, I needed clothes and you clothed me, I was sick and you looked after me, I was in prison and you came to visit me."

In verse forty, he says, "I tell you the truth, whatever you did for one of the least of these brothers of mine, you did for me."

In James 2:17, the author writes, "In the same way, faith by itself, if it is not accompanied by action, is dead."

James 2:24 says, "You see that a person is justified by what he does and not by faith alone."

If we end our relationship with God at our own front door, and never go into the world filled with the Spirit, performing acts of kindness and sharing God's message, as Jesus would, we are being both selfish and unfaithful to the one who taught us.

One purpose of having a special bond with God is to bless those around us and make a positive impact on the lives of others. While my focus has been on our relation to God, the benefits spill over into human relationships. When we improve our relationship with God, we will improve our relationships with people.

People Doing Their Thing

One of the most important lessons I learned over the past couple of years is how difficult it is to make people aware of God. God has many needs on earth, and *we* offer many different opportunities for him to reach out to people. We all have unique talents and, therefore, a unique calling from God.

Insight: "I will speak to each of you directly. When you have heard, act on the words you hear. I will give the assurance that you have done My Will. If this assurance does not come, you may rightly question whether you have heard Me or not."[21]

* * *

St. Augustine, Florida, founded in 1565, claims to be the oldest city in America. The historic section of town includes several quaint streets of cobblestone, the oldest wooden schoolhouse, a seventeenth-century fort, the fountain of youth, and an old jail. It is a high foot traffic tourist area, with small boutique retail stores sprinkled among restaurants, ice-cream shops, and novelty vendors.

During a recent visit to the city, I was intrigued to see a man patrolling the cobblestones carrying a seven-foot wooden cross on his back! Yep, handing out Christian leaflets and talking about Jesus.

Imagine the calling this individual felt to begin this ministry! What an unusual approach! He was reaching out to folks, one person at a time. What a brave man, strapped to a huge cross, heading to the tourist section of town on a Saturday afternoon to preach, to make people aware.

* * *

Soon after learning Christians can also play hard-rock music, I acquired an affinity for one up-and-coming quartet. My son and I attended one of their concerts in downtown Rochester. The lineup included four other popular, secular rock bands.

Each of the warm-up bands played for about thirty minutes leading up to the two secular headliners. My Christian band was one of those warm-up bands. They came onstage in the middle of the night to little reception.

I would not characterize this crowd as a Christian audience. My band was definitely not preaching to the choir. They did, however, play an unforgettably brilliant set of songs; enthusiastic, artistic, and they left the audience agape, in shock. Following their set, the lead singer praised Jesus, and they left the stage.

The next band was the first headliner. Their grand entrance was followed by a plethora of foul language wrapped with a bad attitude. For some reason, the lead singer did not appreciate his reception from the crowd, sang one song, spewed more expletives, and stormed off stage.

The audience stood in disbelief as the guitarists played stall music, while the rest of the band left to find the lead singer. He returned later and, seemingly begrudgingly, finished the set to a chorus of boos.

The main event followed this circus with a respectful show, but we left halfway through their set. We were underwhelmed by all the performances after the Christian group.

We witnessed God's challenge to build awareness in this world. He must penetrate all the crevices of this earth to bring a glimpse of the good news to those who otherwise would be oblivious to the message!

I never realized this difficulty and the efforts being made by people to fulfill God's purpose. Kudos to the underdog Christian rockers who outplayed and outclassed the field that night! They have since become one of the most popular Christian rock bands in the world.

God confirmed my observation:

You witnessed the perfect example of the challenges in fulfilling my purpose. Playing in a hostile environment, surrounded by today's hardened youth.

Bringing witness in the only acceptable form to this group, hard-rock music, with tremendous confidence and showmanship. Witnesses in my name will be persecuted by others, ridiculed, demeaned, and made to feel unworthy. This is evidence of the evil in the world. It takes a strong personality to remain obedient and pursue fulfilling my purpose. It requires faith to stand up to evil and witness.

Be Humble!

When you discover your purpose, in all you do, stay humble, or God will humble you.

* * *

In 2005, my partners and I founded a retail car dealership in Rochester. In 2007, we built three more dealerships down the East Coast. Due to the fast pace of revenue growth, our company was recognized by the Rochester Business Alliance as the city's fastest-growing privately held company. This was a big accomplishment.

At the time, my partner was the CEO, and I was the CFO. We were honored at a luncheon at the city's convention center, with hundreds of Rochester executives in attendance. I prepared a short speech, which included thanking God.

In God's typical style, though, my name was only briefly mentioned in the Saturday newspaper, and it was spelled wrong! In church the following morning, the humor of the situation struck me during a sermon on humility. God told me I needed to be humbled. He gave me a little credit, with a twist. I was allowed to be proud, but not of myself.

† "When pride comes, then comes disgrace, but with humility comes wisdom." (Prov 11:2)

* * *

More recently I was named a finalist for Business Person of the Year by the Small Business Council of Rochester, another event held at the convention center for the five nominees in my category. I was seated at the head table, with the other honorees and dignitaries, elevated on a podium facing eight hundred or so executive attendees, when the emcee introduced me as Ted Hoagey. I looked at my guest table to see all eight of my friends and family laughing. I had to laugh too.

* * *

Life brings many lessons in pride, humility, and dependence on God. If your intent is to glorify God, then glorification will come. Success will come if success will glorify God. All good blessings come from God, not from one's self. When God calls for your fulfillment of purpose, reply respectfully, humbly, and dutifully, and *you*, too, will be fulfilled.

God the Employer

I've heard people respond to an ethical dilemma by asking, "What would Jesus do?" Let's face it; we are humans, so that's not a realistic proposition. But it is *not* unrealistic to evaluate our behavior as if Jesus were standing beside us all day long! How would Jesus feel about our performance at work, about our interaction with others at the water cooler, about our attitude as parents, and our willingness to help with chores around the house?

As Christians, our work ethic and performance should be a reflection of God. As we look to fulfill God's purpose in our lives, we must approach our commitment with this degree of resolve.

All the folks I witness fulfilling God's purpose for their lives are passionate about their mission, ministering in their own way, and doing what they can to glorify God.

† "Whatever you do, work at it with all your heart, as working for the Lord, not for men." (Col 3:23)

How would we approach earthly tasks differently using Colossians 3:23 as a guide? How differently would we perform everyday tasks if God had asked us to do the task instead of man?

If God asked me to build a doghouse, it would be the best doghouse ever built. I would not cut corners. Cost would be no object. I would carefully plan the design, use the best materials, measure twice, cut once, and construct the perfect doghouse. As Christians, we should approach all work in this fashion. This is how we honor God in all we do.

My friend in St. Augustine with the cross was uncompromising; he wasn't suggesting we accept Jesus! He was carrying around a seven-foot cross, handing out leaflets and preaching like the world was about to end. He was demanding awareness, working like Jesus was right beside him! He was working for the Lord, not for man.

Glorify me in everything you do, and you will continue to sense fulfillment; the feeling of a job well done. By testifying in my name, I can affect people I need to affect. You may never become aware, you may never see or hear any accolades, but we are rejoicing in heaven.

God's Special Blessings

God knows how our lives are linked with others, how our answered prayers could leave another's unanswered. We've heard, "Everything happens for a reason." When God has anointed a specific project, events definitely happen for a reason.

Can we fully understand spiritual anointing? This spiritual empowerment is rarely discussed. I believe it is real. Sometimes God's window of opportunity only lasts for a certain period. He may try to show us the right decision, show us the path, give us the answers, but we may not be ready for those answers, and the anointing goes away.

Insight: "When God reveals to you an issue that needs to be dealt with in your life, you can trust that the anointing is also present to break the yoke of its bondage over you. If you put off confronting the behavior until you want to deal with it, you may have to face change without the anointing."[22]

Anointings have expiration dates. This doesn't mean God is going to give up on us; he understands our hesitation. But the perfect alignment God prepared fades away because of our indecision, and we must go back to the drawing board.

Other times we try to force God's anointing, performing his work before his timing. If the caterpillar in the cocoon knew what he was waiting for, would he have the patience to wait? If God revealed his purpose for our life, wouldn't we try to achieve it on our clock? Most likely before we are ready?

How would I explain the anointing if you hadn't experienced both the anointing and its absence? Now you know how it feels by comparison. You know how to receive. Ask in prayer, in daily prayer.

Fulfillment of God's purpose with his anointing is much easier than working on our own without his anointing. I have felt God's anointing, and I also know when I do not have it.

Daily prayer increases the possibility of his anointing and the opportunity to keep it flowing. Pray for God to reveal his blessed purpose for your life and for his anointing to fulfill it!

You Will Be Ready!

Insight: "You are far too important to God for him to squander your talents or misplace you. In fact, you are so precious to him that he has hidden you close to him, to polish and perfect your spiritual gifts. He is waiting for the right moment—the right assignment—to send you soaring."[23]

Insight: "The desire you have to serve God comes from him. Do not be afraid how you will serve. He will provide you with everything you need, and he will accomplish amazingly good things through you."[24]

Insight: "You are being led in a very definite way, and others, who do not serve your purpose, are being moved out of your Path by Me. Never fear, whatever may happen…Do not try to plan. I have planned. You are the builder, not the architect."[25]

Writing a book was the furthest thing from my mind when I moved to the lake and began jotting notes in a private journal. I was searching for my own salvation. I could never have foreseen the volumes of material God would reveal to me.

I became secure in my relationship with God over time, but I was terribly insecure witnessing to others. Maybe this stemmed from my issues with worthiness. I heard others offering advice, interpreting scripture and preaching with such conviction and confidence that I felt very inadequate.

I began to interact with other Christians. We shared similar stories, and I could sense a kindred spirit with folks who otherwise shared no common interests. I realized my contribution would be experiential, not educational, and my experiences with God would make my story unique and worth sharing. No one can tell me I am wrong, because these are my personal experiences!

Writing a book, however, loomed as a commitment of a much higher level. I was an executive of a large company, and I knew nothing about writing a book, nor did I have many hours to spare. But I knew enough about God's timing and had confidence in our relationship after so many coincidences, visions, and teachings, that I was willing to follow his direction.

Whether the following scripture should have been my validation or not to write a book, at the time, it seemed clear God gave it to me for this reason.

✝ "Then the Lord replied, 'Write down the revelation and make it plain on tablets so that a herald [whoever reads it] may run with it. For the revelation awaits an appointed time; it speaks of the end and will not prove false. Though it linger, wait for it; it will certainly come and will not delay.'" (Hab 2:2–3)

I am sharing the following prayers after realizing I was meant to tell my story and become a witness, somehow, someway, with the reassurance God will provide for me:

* * *

"I do not fear your will for my life any longer. I do not fear your will is sacrificial, scary, or unattainable. I have confidence your will for my life can be achieved. I am ready to pursue that fulfillment now.

"You know I need a purpose, and I need to be challenged. You also know I require a lot of reinforcement and encouragement. I am young, insecure in this new venture. I am learning the game. I see how significant the opponent is, but I don't know what position you want me to play. I want to get into the game and make an impact.

"Show me, lead me, tell me. You know I am skeptical and stubborn, so if you have someone to help me fulfill this purpose, you should make him obvious."

* * *

"Today, I am excited. I progressed from having a morning of desperation yesterday to an afternoon of hope and inspiration today. You answered my prayer from yesterday, seeking reassurance:

> Now you have been given the assignment. You realize the size of the task. Do not be overwhelmed. You have a lifetime of material, and you have what is most important—faith."

* * *

"I felt a sense of urgency to learn about hell. I read an entire book about hell in one night. The following morning, I heard from you on the subject, and at night I had dinner with a good friend who, I learned through an unusual discussion about spirituality, did not believe in hell. Boy, did I give him an earful, and I bought him two books about hell for Christmas. How perfect is your timing!"

This is proof when the time comes, you will be ready.

* * *

"Thank you, Lord, for showing me how easy it can be to witness. You will arm me with the knowledge and experiences to properly communicate your message. You will create opportunities and place them before me. You will give me the strength to speak on your behalf with conviction."

THE FINAL CHAPTER— WRAPPING IT UP

Don't Look Back

What caused the troubles in your life? Are you focused on the problems, on a transgression from the past, or on the forgiveness and mercy of God? Are you consumed with moving buckets under the leaky roof or interested in fixing the foundation and building a beautiful house?

We have regrets over past actions. Hindsight is perfect; we are not. I had a very big debt canceled. My life is a trail of misgivings and close calls. I should have known better. I became aware of God at an early age and certainly had enough guidance over the years to avoid the mistakes I made. I would have been much more valuable to God had I paid attention to him earlier in my life.

God is not pleased with divorce; he is not pleased if we commit a crime or break a commandment. He is probably not pleased with many of the decisions we make, but that does not make our situations hopeless! Learn from these experiences. If we turn to God, these circumstances can strengthen our relationship with him, and they can lead to great ministering opportunities.

My biggest mistake was not knowing God and not allowing him an opportunity to guide my life when I needed him. It became cliché for me to hear, "Give your concerns to God, and he will provide the solution." I did not really believe his help was available. I did not know how real he is. Unlike you, I did not have the benefit of this documented journey for guidance.

When I asked God to cure my feelings of unworthiness, he did. I could not identify the source of my leaky roof, praying to God to reveal the fundamental flaw preventing my happiness. I don't know how or when I overcame my tireless quest for acceptance, but it is gone.

Maybe my acceptance by God completely overshadowed my need for earthly worthiness. I may never understand how, but I'm certain if he had not fixed my roof, I would still be moving buckets today.

Use Me as I Am, Sooner Better Than Perfect

I am far from a model Christian. I wasn't when I set out on this journey, and I am not one today. But I am light-years ahead of where I was, and I know God is still working on me; my adventure is only beginning. My experience will be ongoing, far beyond these lessons, and he will be with me on earth until we meet in heaven.

As I complete this chapter, I have been writing and typing for eleven years. God never told me the book would be written overnight. I write at night, I write on airplanes, I write whenever I have a minute. God makes the time for me and gives me the motivation to keep going. It is a lot of work, but it is not a hardship. I enjoy every minute. It brings me peace.

I have no idea where my life will lead now that I'm finished with this book, but I think it is going to be good. I'm not concerned whether I feel ready for God's next step, because I'm certain he will prepare me.

I anticipate criticism. I read online skepticism about books like mine, proclaiming messages from God. Some reviews are downright mean. There are also many comments from people who understand, and by people whose lives are saved by God's inspiring words. I have done my best to deliver his messages, and I will be satisfied if I bring only one person to Jesus.

May this book be a blessing in your life. May you use it to further your intimacy with God, find your purpose, and witness to others in your own special way.

It's Your Turn Now!

I hope this message has been clear—develop a relationship with God, and his path will be obvious. He will walk with you every inch of the way.

We all have different experiences to share, different talents to share. Do not hesitate to ask God how you can use your abilities to further his kingdom. If you already know, don't be afraid to act!

Do not compare your love, your righteousness, your worthiness to me, or others. It doesn't matter. Internalize this guidebook and God's messages and pursue your relationship with him now, not thirty years from now.

Don't listen to anyone who says you are not worthy. Their opinions are not important! Don't be intimidated by anyone. Care only about God's opinion.

If God is in your life, he will glorify it in ways you cannot believe. Follow the road map of spiritual milestones. Build a relationship with him. This relationship will become companionship. Find God's purpose for your life and fulfill it!

We received our salvation, now let's do our best to honor this gift!

Thank you, Father. Alleluia. Amen.

ENDNOTES

1. A. J. Russell, *God Calling* (Uhrichsville, OH: Barbour Publishing, 1989), August 6.
2. *Listen, the Lord, Instructions in Spiritual Awareness and Interior Prayer, as Given to Seven Who Hear* (Santa Fe, NM: Rydal Press, 1956), 88.
3. Russell, *God Calling*, February 6.
4. *Listen, the Lord*, 134.
5. R. A. Torrey, *How to Pray* (New Kensington, PA: Whitaker House, 1984), 26.
6. Russell, *God Calling*, August 19.
7. Bill Hybels, *Too Busy Not to Pray* (Downers Grove, IL: InterVarsity Press, 2008), 29.
8. Hybels, *Too Busy Not to Pray*, 134.
9. Stephen M. Miller, *The Jesus of the Bible* (Uhrichsville, OH: Barbour Publishing, 2009), 176.
10. Russell, *God Calling*, February 22.
11. Russell, *God Calling*, February 22.
12. Russell, *God Calling*, September 17.
13. Russell, *God Calling*, September 18.
14. *Listen, the Lord*, 67.
15. *Listen, the Lord*, 32.
16. Russell, *God Calling*, June 12.
17. *Moments of Peace for the Morning* (Bloomington, MN: Bethany House Publishers, 2009), 38.
18. *Listen, the Lord*, 122.
19. *Listen, the Lord*, 24.
20. *Listen, the Lord*, 24.
21. *Listen, the Lord*, 31.
22. Joyce Meyer, *How to Hear from God* (Nashville: FaithWords, 2008), 105.
23. *Moments of Peace for the Morning*, 28.
24. *Moments of Peace for the Morning*, 152.
25. Russell, *God Calling*, January 29.

www.ingramcontent.com/pod-product-compliance
Lightning Source LLC
Chambersburg PA
CBHW071228080526
44587CB00013BA/1542